"This book is about love, human love. Our love for each other. Love for this incredibly exciting and beautiful world. Love for the precious gift of self. And God's love for us."

—Marjorie Holmes

To Phyllis
with love

Eileen

May 14, 1981

Bantam Books by Marjorie Holmes
Ask your bookseller for the books you have missed

BEAUTY IN YOUR OWN BACKYARD
HOLD ME UP A LITTLE LONGER, LORD
HOW CAN I FIND YOU, GOD?
I'VE GOT TO TALK TO SOMEBODY, GOD
LORD, LET ME LOVE
LOVE AND LAUGHTER
NOBODY ELSE WILL LISTEN
TWO FROM GALILEE
WHO AM I, GOD?

LORD, LET ME LOVE

A Marjorie Holmes Treasury

Drawings by Maryanne Regal Hoburg

TORONTO · BANTAM BOOKS · LONDON
NEW YORK

LORD, LET ME LOVE
A Bantam Book / published by arrangement with
Doubleday & Co., Inc.

PRINTING HISTORY
Doubleday edition published July 1978
4 printings through February 1980
A Doubleday Book Club Selection November 1978
A Selection of Christian Herald Family Bookshelf
July and August 1979
Serialized in Faith and Inspiration, April 1979.
Bantam edition / June 1981

ACKNOWLEDGMENTS

Grateful acknowledgment is made by the author to the editors of the following magazines, newspapers and publishers where many of these prayers and poems first appeared, for permission to reprint:

"'What Became of the Man I Married?'" reprinted from Better Homes & Gardens. *Copyright 1952 by Meredith Corp. All rights reserved.*

"A Song of Praise for Spring," "Give Me a Generous Spirit," "Bathtime," "The New Outfit," "Help Me to Unclutter My Life," "Shopping with a Daughter," "The Stoning," "Good Roots," "'If Only,'" "Paper Boy," "For Being Cherished," "The Generous Artistry," "Fortify Me with Memories," "Let Me Go Gently," "The Courage to Be Kind," "Bless My Good Intentions," "Hold Me Up a Little Longer," "Don't Let Me Take It for Granted," "Time Out for Love," "Possessions," "The Son Who Won't Study," "Let Them Remember Laughter," "Getting at It," "Let Me Take Time for Beauty," "This House to Keep," "Don't Let Me Stop Growing," "Needlework Prayer," "Forgiving Means Forgetting," "Let Me Say 'Yes' to New Experiences," "I'm Tired of Being Strong," "The Missing Ingredient," "I Can't Understand My Daughter Any More," "The Box in the Attic," "Give Me the Love to Let Them Go," "I Must Depend on Myself," "A Mother's Wish—Gifts for Christmas," "New Year's Eve," "An American Woman's Prayer" (first appeared in Ladies' Home Journal as "An American Woman's Bicentennial Prayer"), *from* Hold Me Up a Little Longer, Lord, *copyright © 1971, 1972, 1973, 1974, 1975, 1976, 1977, by Marjorie Holmes Mighell. Published by Doubleday & Company, Inc., and reprinted by permission.*

"The Cows," "Cut Back the Vines," "The Earth's Heart Beating," "For Every Cross I've Carried," "God Says 'Get Up!'" "Let No Job Be Beneath Me," "More Stately Mansions," "Music," "Poetry," "A Potato," "The Suffering Few of Us Escape," "To Love, to Labor," "The Trees," "Two by the Side of the Road," "Why Am I Working Here?" "With the Tongues of Men and Angels," "His Very World Dances," *from* How Can I Find You, God? *copyright © 1975 by Marjorie Holmes Mighell. Published by Doubleday & Company, Inc., and reprinted by permission.*

"A Mother's Prayer in the Morning" as "Mother's Prayer at Morning," "Night Duty" as "Mother Answers Voice in Night," "Order" as "Psalm for an Apron Pocket," "Bring Back the Children" as "A Mother's Arms Aren't Long Enough," *copyright © 1966, 1967, 1968, by The Evening Star Newspaper Company.* "I've Got to Talk to Somebody, God," "I've Said 'Yes' Once too Often," "I'm Showing My Age," "I Was So Cross to the Children," "For a Wanted Child," "For an Unexpected Child," "Respite," "Scrubbing a Floor," "Unexpected Company," "The Refrigerator," "The Tender Trap," "The Hour of Love," "The Quarrel," "When a Husband Loses Interest," "The Good Days of Marriage," "A Psalm for Marriage," "Self-pity," "Give Me Patience," "My Body," "The Compliment," "Just for Today," "A Boy's First Car," "Going to Church with a Daughter," "Rescue This Child," "The Garden," "When the Winds Cry I Hear You," *from* I've Got to Talk to Somebody, God, *copyright © 1968, 1969, by Marjorie Holmes Mighell. Published by Doubleday & Company, Inc., and reprinted by permission.*

"The Buffet Drawer," "A Child's Hand in Yours," "Good-by, Christmas Tree," "Her Ark and Her Covenant," "The Letter Home," "Little Boys," "Mother, I'm Home," "The Runaway Canoe," "Little Girls Together," *copyright © 1964, 1965, by The Evening Star Newspaper Company;* "Mothers Keep All These Things" *© 1964, 1965, by The Evening Star Newspaper Company.* "Mothers Keep All These Things" *appeared in* Today's Health, *copyright © 1966, 1967, by American Medical Association.* "'What Became of the Girl I Married?'" reprinted from Better Homes & Gardens *and* Reader's Digest, *copyright 1952 by Meredith Corp. All are from* Love and Laughter, *published by Doubleday & Company, Inc., and reprinted by permission.*

ISBN 0-553-14915-6

Published simultaneously in the United States and Canada

Bantam Books are published by Bantam Books, Inc. Its trademark, consisting of the words "Bantam Books" and the portrayal of a bantam, is Registered in U.S. Patent and Trademark Office and in other countries. Marca Registrada. Bantam Books, Inc., 666 Fifth Avenue, New York, New York 10103.

PRINTED IN THE UNITED STATES OF AMERICA

0 9 8 7 6 5 4 3 2 1

For my love sisters
Alice Holmes
and
Yula Parker

Lord,
Let Me Love

Contents

YOUNG LOVE

MARRIED LOVE

FAMILY LOVE

LIFE LOVE

SELF LOVE

GOD LOVE

Preface

This book is about love.

Human love. Our love for each other. Love for this incredibly exciting and beautiful world. Love for the precious gift of self. And God's love for us.

It is composed of selections that have appeared in magazines or some of my previous books. Pieces that readers tell me *they* have loved.

Putting it together was a joyous but in some ways painful labor of love. So many pieces begged to be included, so many had to be left out. (It was a little like having to shut the door on your own children.)

I hope you will find your favorites here, or others you missed but now can love. For it is through words, spoken or written, that the circles of love widen, or that we touch and share more deeply the true meaning of life with those we love.

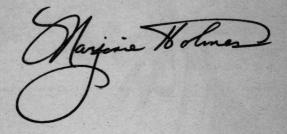

*Young
Love*

When I'm a Mother, Will I?

Lord, when I'm a mother will I . . .

Try to pick my daughter's boy friends, and always think that those who dress and talk and act the nicest around a girl's parents are the ones you can trust, the ones who'll be best for her? . . .

Want her to be best friends with daughters of *my* friends, and with cousins she can't stand? . . .

Worry when she doesn't have dates, and worry when she *does*? And wait up and ask for explanations when she comes in late?

Lord, when I'm a mother will I tell her how much harder I had things when I was growing up, and what a considerate, generous, helpful, obedient daughter I always was?

Will I forget all the bad parts of being my age now and remember all the good parts and try to mold my daughter into some beautiful memory of myself?

Lord, will I make as many mistakes with my daughter as I think my mother makes with me?

I suppose I will, Lord. But whatever I do, just let me love her as much as I know my mother loves me.

He Thinks I'm Beautiful

Oh, Lord, he thinks I'm beautiful! This boy thinks I'm beautiful. At least that's what he says, and when I look in the mirror I think he could be right.

My eyes are shining, my hair is lively and shining too, my smile is suddenly brighter. I'm standing straighter, and I feel —oh, lovely and strangely alluring. I feel graceful. Even my clothes look better on me.

I feel, and suddenly believe I am, some of the things I've always longed to be—at least attractive, worth looking at.

Thank you, Lord, for this awareness of loveliness in myself. I want to be beautiful for him. I *will* be beautiful for him— and for all the other people I'm going to meet in life.

I will be beautiful for this boy and for those other people, yes. But also—for myself. It gives me so much self-confidence, it makes me feel so good. The whole world looks wonderfully different.

Thank you for this transformation. (Help me to hang onto it even if he looks a little closer and changes his mind!) Thank you that for once in my life I am beautiful in somebody's sight.

To Walk in Beauty

No garment is more becoming
than love. No vitamin more invigorating.
No lotion, potion, or cosmetic more
glamorizing. The exciting secret of true
beauty is love.

Some say that when beauty fades, love
goes. Isn't it the other way around?
Beauty only fades when love is gone.

In you would walk in beauty, stay
in love! You will see the loved one as
beautiful. You will see yourself as
beautiful. All the world about you will be
beautiful. And the people in that world
will seem more beautiful, for they will
reflect the shining warmth and beauty
you radiate.

The Betrothal

He, Joseph, had only his love for Mary. She was his Temple, his wealth and his wisdom. And to her he would bring all that he possessed, every stitch, every penny, every eagerly hewn bit of wood. Every fiber of his strong young body, every thought that did not first belong to him who had made her for him, their God.

He was awed by the honor of his undertaking, but he was not humbled. He knew that the gift of total commitment is never small.

Joseph worked feverishly even the day of his betrothal. It would help to pass the hours until sundown. Furthermore, there had been a slight upsurge of business, as if already his union with the house of Joachim might become an asset to his family. He did not want to be found wanting, and he wanted to prosper. Soon he would have a wife to support.

Suddenly he could not believe it. The daze of sheer blind yielding, moving forward, ever forward in harmony with his fate deserted him. Something might happen even yet. Hannah might still hurl herself between them. Or some awful caprice of God might strike. His mother had gone up to help with the baking; any moment she might rush in, her eyes cold with horror. Or Timna would never return at all. The day would simply go on forever, with Mary ahead of him like a mirage on the desert, or a port toward which he was forever doomed to sail.

"My darling, you're still working?" His mother's hand

parted the curtains, her concerned face peered through. "It's growing late, I'll fetch the water for your bath and lay out your garments." Flushed and perspiring but smiling, she pulled off her kerchief. Hannah had bade her come up with the aunts and other kin to join in the joyous preparations. Kneading the dough and baking it in the ovens dug in the yard, setting out the vegetables that were now bursting in such abundance, polishing the bright fruit, checking the wine. And all the while they worked, caught up in the glittering net of women's talk. They had praised each other's efforts and each other's children, favoring her especially, as mother of the groom.

Home now, she looked about with her familiar anxiety for her husband. But Jacob was fine, Joseph assured her; only sleeping. "Good," she sighed, "he'll need the rest. We'll be up late. You should have rested too." She pressed his arm.

Joseph bathed and dressed and anointed his hair with olive oil. His confidence was returning. As the water had washed away the grime and sweat, so it cleansed him of his nervous, foolish imaginings. He felt the splendor of his own body in its pure white linen; he felt the wonder of his youth pulsing, urgent and eager. One small thing troubled him exceedingly—his hands. Although he scrubbed them nearly raw and rubbed them with the precious oil, he could do nothing about their callouses or the scarred, broken nails. He wanted to be perfect for Mary. He did not want his hands to be harsh, clasping hers, or to snag the betrothal veil.

His father puffed in and out, bumping into him, borrowing things, asking Joseph's help with the tying of his girdle. Jacob could never manage and his wife was busy with the girls. "And do I have to wear shoes?" he pleaded, exhibiting his poor swollen feet with their bunions. Squat, ruddy, his wispy hair combed futilely over his baldness, he looked uncomfortably clean and dressed up and rather pathetic. Yet it was he who reminded Joseph of the things that in his agitation he might forget: the purse of long-hoarded silver dinars, the ring, the presents.

Together they set off at last, Joseph lugging the heavy table. Jacob limped along in his unaccustomed sandals. A brisk breeze set the palm trees clashing and blew their robes about their legs. The dusty cobbled streets seemed strangely empty, as if life had been suspended for this gravely impending hour. Behind a tumbled-down rock fence a camel lurched growling to his feet, a donkey worried a bucket and brayed. They trudged along the steep narrow corridors in a strange silence. They were miserably aware, the nearer they drew to their destination, of the inadequacy of their offerings.

Ahead of them in the fast falling darkness they saw the newly whitened bridal house in its clump of prickly pears. Fluttering from it like a beckoning arm was the pennant that proclaimed its festivities to passers-by. As they approached they saw that Joachim had stepped outside to light the torch of pitch-soaked rushes at the step. It blazed up suddenly, revealing his face with its unguarded look of grief. However quickly he jerked his head there was no denying that naked sorrowing. Because of me? Joseph wondered, or only because his dearest child has so little time left to be under his roof? Promptly Joachim recovered himself and turned to welcome them. Courteously ignoring the gifts they carried, he led them inside.

The room had been transformed. This was no house now, but Eden; the women had gathered up armsful of Eden and brought it inside. The white walls struggled to hold up its colors—the shining green of dampened leaves, and blossoms that rose in a bright riot, to wind even into the rushes of the ceiling. Purple iris, scarlet carnations, pink and blue cyclamen, the ruddy cups of tulips, heavy-headed poppies, already beginning to swoon in the heat of the lamps that stood like little floating stars.

The largest lamp, burning the finest oil, was placed at the head of the table where the bride and groom were led. Joseph found himself there as in a dream. Mary seemed unreal beside him, though her sweet flesh at times brushed against his. The scent of her was more heady than the overpowering fragrance of the flowers. He was stiff with guarding his emotions, remote from her, afraid. Her eyes had a fixed shining, she was smiling, smiling, laughing and smiling before the lavish compliments that each guest paid as he laid his gifts at her feet. Bolts of cloth, baskets, jugs, skeins of flax, countless tools for keeping house. The guests deposited them and then returned to their seats which were bedecked with olive boughs.

Finally an expectant hush; the scribe came forward. The rabbi nodded to Joseph, whose heart was large in his throat. With unsteady hands he drew from his girdle the purse containing the marriage fee, and turned to Mary, whose face floated before him. Not smiling now, but grave and as white as one of the pure white roses in her crown.

"And have you brought a token to give the bride to signify that this covenant is made?"

Nodding, Joseph unwound his girdle. His eyes did not leave Mary's as the rabbi took it and placed it across her uplifted hands.

"And have you other gifts?" the rabbi asked.

"Yes." If only there were more. . . . But nobody seemed to think ill of them, the shawl he had for Hannah, the fine hand chisel for Joachim. And for Mary—ah, for Mary, the sewing box, the soft little doeskin slippers, and the table that would be the first piece of furniture for their house. Plainly she loved them all, especially the slippers. She cried out with delight and thrust out her feet to their measure. There was an awkward moment for it seemed as if she would have him kneel there in the presence of everyone to put them on her. He flushed and people laughed at his discomfort and the rabbi made stern noises in his throat. For the scribe sat waiting to pen the terms of the contract.

And when it was finished, Joseph spoke aloud the prescribed words: that he would work for her and honor her in the manner of Jewish husbands, and that all of his property would be hers forever. Thus did he openly take the vow already made within his heart.

It was over now, all but the draping of her face with the betrothal veil. But the children must first be called forward. They had been bouncing with impatience for their treats; now the rabbi beckoned, and the mothers who had been restraining them let them go. They came in an eager swarm, shrieking, hands outstretched for the nuts and cakes. The eyes of Mary and Joseph met, and between them ran a shining thread of wonder, for despite its festive nature, this too was a grave thing, this matter of bestowing the sweets. For it symbolized the fact that she had kept herself for him.

In the commotion he almost forgot the veil. "The veil, the veil!" various ones were whispering. "Quiet the children." An aunt shepherded most of them outside, the others clung to their mothers, eyes focused with a placid interest on the bride.

As Joseph had feared, his fingers caught on the delicate gossamer stuff, and his hands shook placing it with anguished care so that it fell before her face. Yet pride upheld him. This was his victory; he knew that he stood before them tall and comely, humble yet mighty, a man claiming his true bride.

A vast tenderness swept him, and a great reverence. Now she belonged to him and her face was his to shield. In regret and joy he draped her, his personal Torah, which now must be returned to the ark to await their covenant.

Mary could not sleep. Affectionately she had thanked her parents for the betrothal feast and bade them goodnight and crept into the chamber from which they had removed the younger children, in deference to her new state. Long before the revelry was over the little ones had collapsed one by one, to be carried, limp as the drooping flowers, to pallets in various corners of the house. There, heavy with food and spent with excitement, they slept the deep sleep of the innocent. Her parents slept too at last! She had lain rigid during the long hour when they had murmured together. But finally the voices and the creaking of the mattress ceased. There was heavy silence broken only by Joachim's snores.

Slowly, luxuriantly, she let her knotted fists uncurl, her whole being go limp. And as she did so the memories came flooding in . . . Joseph. *Joseph!* The proud tilt of his head throughout the ceremony. The trembling of his hands—she marveled that he hadn't dropped things as he had once dropped the towel. She ached for him; all that he did was inordinately precious and must be looked at in the fresh new light of herself, alone in her chamber and yet bound to him, awaiting their hour.

And it was all mixed up with that longing which made her toss and turn, which is why she had held herself back until her parents slept . . . Joseph! The grave little smile upon his face as people shouted blessings and wished them well. And his eyes upon her in the glare of the torches in the garden. Those passionate, pensive gray eyes. And the songs that he had sung only for her, quietly, next to her at the feast table, looking straight ahead almost as if she were not present. Singing to her softly, secretly, wooing her with his lips and his remoteness while the others danced and sang.

> *"Thou hast ravished my heart, my sister, my spouse; thou hast ravished my heart with one of thine eyes. . . . How fair is thy love, my sister, my spouse! how much better is thy love than wine! . . ."*

Some of the village boys had brought up lutes and a timbrel, and they too sang and danced, but like shadows, a spectral chorus whose faces flared and fell in the roistering light. Abner had been among them, a trifle tipsy with wine even before he came, striding about making noise, which was alien to his shy nature, and by that giving his heartbreak away. Poor Abner. And poor Cleophas, who had gone off to console himself in Magdala, she had learned. She grieved for them, yet always her being turned back to Joseph. He was the only one she had ever wanted, and he was hers. Hers by law. If he were to die she would be his widow. And if she were to die he would be her widower. And if she were to betray him he would have to give her a bill of divorcement.

But no—no, how could she entertain such thoughts on this night of her betrothal when the moon was shining for good luck? It was still fairly early; the working people of Nazareth could not spend much of the night in celebration, for they had to rise at dawn. The moon was still so bright they had scarcely needed torches going home. It was flooding her little room and she couldn't bear it, this restlessness, fed by the moonlight.

By night on my bed I sought him whom my soul loveth; I sought him, but I found him not.

I will rise now, and go about the city in the streets, and in the broad ways I will seek him whom my soul loveth. . . .

She found herself at the window. The moon possessed the sky. It traced every tree and twig and bush and branch in silver, laying inky shadows, giving everything a stark clarity seldom seen by day. "Joseph. *Joseph!*" she whispered toward that blandly smiling and triumphant face. Was he sleepless too, perhaps pacing alone in this unutterable light, or gazing up in a frenzy of longing? And all because she had indeed set forth on the streets like the bride in Solomon's dream:

. . . but I found him whom my soul loveth: I held him, and would not let him go, until I had brought him into my mother's house, and into the chamber of her that conceived me. . . .

My dove, my perfect one, is only one, the darling of her mother. . . .

Hannah. Poor brave beaten little Hannah, who had been finally reconciled. Who slept in the next room by her husband's side. While the bride . . . the groom? Mary shuddered and pressed her hands to her breasts.

"A *garden enclosed in my sister, my spouse,*" Joseph had gone on singing from those selfsame songs, "*a spring shut up, a fountain sealed.*"

Joseph. Joseph. She gave herself over to the final memory, held back to savor utterly. The moment in the garden when both her mother and father had been busy with the guests and they two had drawn a little apart. He had gripped both her hands within his own. "Would to heaven this were our wedding night!"

"Yes. Yes," she whispered, swaying toward him. "But we must be patient, and it won't be long, I promise. Just as I persuaded my father before, I'll surely be able to persuade him not to postpone the wedding for long."

Yet even as they gazed at each other in the nakedness of their yearning, she had begun to shrink from the task ahead. Having yielded thus far, her parents might feel it a point of honor not to yield again. Besides, they loved her, she was their firstborn. She knew that they would keep her with them as long as possible.

Journey of Discovery

*Every experience in love is a journey
of self-discovery. The more we
learn about the one we love the more we
learn about ourselves. And even though
the love may cool and we may go our
separate ways, we have gained in
knowledge. We understand at least one
other person better. And we cannot help
but better understand that intriguing,
groping, puzzling companion we are
destined to live with forever: the secret
inner self.*

*Strangely—fortunately—seemingly
unlovable people do have those who
love them. But only the lovable and
loving ever enjoy the true delight and
wonder of love.*

*I don't think love is "never having to say
you're sorry." If we're human we all hurt
each other—even when we don't mean to.
True love is understanding and being
willing to say, "I'm sorry."*

Married
Love

A Psalm for Marriage

I am married, I am married, and my heart is glad.

I will give thanks unto the Lord for the love and protection of my husband. I will give thanks for the blessed protection and satisfaction of my home. I will give thanks that I have someone of my own to help and comfort and even to worry about, someone to encourage and to love.

My husband is beside me wherever I need to go. My husband is behind me supporting me in whatever I need to do. I need not face the world alone. I need not face my family alone.

I need face only myself and my God alone. And this is good. This is very good.

Whatever our differences, whatever our trials, I will give thanks unto the Lord for my husband and my marriage. For so long as I have both my husband and my God I am a woman complete, I am not alone.

The Priceless Gift

Lord of life, creator of man and woman, thank you for the priceless gift of sex. Sex as you intended it long ago in the garden at time's beginning, when they saw that they were naked. Innocent, without responsibility, they hadn't realized. But in their hard-won wisdom they saw, and covered themselves.

I don't think it was their shame, God. It was the instinct you gave them, their basic common sense. For the marvel of their differentness was enhanced by the shielding leaves.

They achieved mystery for each other; they achieved a sweet excitement and new worth. And they achieved another very precious thing—personal privacy. The right to keep to oneself the most important part of oneself.

In this way I think you conveyed to man and woman the true wonder and beauty of sex. Secret not because of being shameful but because of its infinite value. Something too significant in the scheme of human happiness to be lightly exposed.

Lord of life, creator of man and woman, thank you for the joyous fulfillment of sex. When this marvelous secret is shared between two people who deeply love each other. Shared freely, generously, completely, without shame.

Thank you for this most perfect of all human delights, most profound of all human communions. This that regenerates both body and spirit.

The most vital act of life, the very core and source of life. Help us to appreciate and revere it always, the priceless gift of sex.

A Woman's Name

Listen, Lord, please listen . . .

I miss myself sometimes, I even miss my name.

How is it, I wonder, that I have become just "Mother," "Mom," or "Honey"? Words that are tender and kindly but simply don't conjure up *me*. The person I really am.

I sometimes long for the sound of my whole given name. And my last name too. The name that first marked me as belonging to my parents, blood of their blood, name of their name.

You know how truly grateful I am to be a good man's wife. Entitled to stand before the world as *Mrs.* Glad that I bear my husband's name. A name of honor and achievement; and that I am proud that he is the summary and epitome of all the qualities of that name.

But isn't something vital lost when, even through marriage, anyone assumes another person's name? Isn't that the first subtle erosion of a woman's identity? To be known no longer as herself but as merely an adjunct to a man?

Cleave to each other, we are told. Become one flesh. And in most matters let the man be master.

I agree with this, Lord. I believe this is not only your will but good sense. However we may rail against it, seek to escape it, it is wise because it is natural. It works. It makes for a stronger home.

Yet how can a woman ever discover her own soul's value if she is nothing but echo and shadow of a man?

Lord, you know I love my husband and cherish the protection and even the status of his name. But don't let me forget who I am. Let me cling to myself, too.

Please don't let me ever lose the precious individuality you created, if only through the simple symbol of my name.

"What Became of the Man I Married?"

There is one luxury that any man, rich or poor, can give his wife. It costs him nothing, yet it is, curiously enough, the one thing that his wife wants more than anything under heaven. But, by some perverse force of fate, it is also the one thing the average American male puts the least stock in.

The American husband has many virtues. He is a good provider. He works faithfully and hard. He buys more insurance against illness, accident, old age and his own demise than any man anywhere in the world. What's more, he is fundamentally loyal. When the telephone rings and a husband sighs, "I won't be home for dinner, dear, I've got to work late," 99 women out of 100 can believe him implicitly.

He can be counted on not only because he's basically decent but also because he's simply too unromantic to kick up his heels. Give him a comfortable home, a place to pursue his hobby, a wife who feeds him well, sympathizes with his problems and takes good care of the children—and home is the one place he'd rather be than anywhere else. And he's usually too busy reading the newspaper or puttering about the basement to notice or care whether or not his dream girl still wears that cute curl and is a svelte size 12. She's with him and he's with her. And that, to him, is proof positive of love.

That this attitude is the direct opposite of every phase of courting never bothers him. As Dorothy Dix said, "when you've caught your streetcar, you don't go on chasing it." Relieved of the frantic need to rush after his heart's desire, he settles down to the business of her support, not even suspecting that he's neglecting her nearest and dearest desire—romantic love.

Yet romantic love is, to every normal woman, quite as important as material security and faithfulness. It is, in most cases, the reason a woman marries in the first place. What man ever won fair maiden by promising, "I will hoe the garden, pay the bills on time and take out life insurance"? No. He pleads, "Darling, I can't live without you. I want you forever in my arms." And she believes it.

Wrapped in this shining cloak of adoration, she is swept ecstatically into marriage. But, unlike the male of the species, she is not content to drop that cloak and start scrubbing the kitchen as all-sufficient proof of her corresponding passion. Her home duties are proof of devotion, but they seldom assume for her the same role that her husband's work does for him—namely, a substitute for ardor. To her, love is a continuing emotional state. It does *not* become simply an established fact when two people join their lives.

The average woman is, I believe, love-conscious and love-anxious at least 60 percent of the time. Nature has designed her to be emotionally responsive, yielding, warm, sympathetic and sensitive. For these are the qualities and emotions that make for motherhood, that go with its very equipment—the womb that shelters, the breast that nourishes, the arms that comfort and carry. And they are also inevitably linked with a woman's major need and function, love.

I realize that there are plenty of stupid wives, nagging wives, wives who become dowdy and dull and break all the well-known rules for holding affection. On the other hand, more women would strive to be stimulating and beautiful if they tasted the sweet heady flavor of adulation more often. Love is a more potent beautifier than any cream, lotion or charm course on the market. Nearly everyone has observed some drab little creature who became downright stunning simply because some man thought her so. And nearly everyone has seen some truly gorgeous woman gradually fade because her man was so unobserving or chary of compliments that beauty itself became joyless and without meaning.

The husbands who really do care about their wives' appearance would find a little old-fashioned flattery doubly rewarding. They'd have partners to be prouder of on Ladies' Day at their luncheon clubs, and they'd actually save money. Lots of women buy clothes they don't need in the vague hope that if they change outfits often enough their husbands will eventually notice they exist. The man who's smart enough to convince his honey she's a knockout in anything she dons isn't likely to find her too bitter about wearing make-do's. No Schiaparelli original can make a female feel so robed in glory as the admiration of the man she loves.

Maybe this doesn't fall under the classification of romantic love. Maybe it's just old-fashioned bread-and-butter married love. But basically it's what every woman wants—to be cherished, to feel herself adored, to be drawn richly and consciously ever closer to her man.

Another thing the average American husband doesn't understand is the way women feel about sex. Women differ in their needs and responsiveness, just as men do. But more women are more passionate than a lot of men suspect, simply because the women are too modest to let on. I don't honestly think, however, that sexual satisfaction is in itself nearly so important to a woman as the feeling of reassurance the relationship gives her—the reaffirmation of the fact that her husband has wanted to be close to her, to hold her in his arms, to be complete with her in a way that shuts the whole world out. Impotence would be a lot less common in men if they could understand that. Women don't so much seek physical thrills and bodily fulfillment as they seek a time and place of nearness, of going spiritually back—just two people alone together—to those far-lost moments of the past when each was supremely important to the other.

If I were a man, I would make it the first and last acts of my day to take my wife a few moments into my arms. I would make this drawing together so much a part of the fabric of our daily lives that either of us would feel lost without it. It would be the symbol of that blind hurtling together we first knew, a moment of closeness and strength exchanged with which to launch the day. And no matter how many other things had come thrusting between us, it would be a final seal of unity and communion at the day's end.

The Hour of Love

Oh, God, thank you for this beautiful hour of love.

My dear is asleep now, but I am too filled with the wonder and joy of it to sleep just yet.

I stand at the window gazing up at your star-riddled sky. I lean on the sill and gaze down upon your quiet earth.

How rich and fruitful it smells, how fragrant with life and the promise of life.

I see your trees reaching out as if to each other. For even trees must have mates to mature. Then they cast down their seeds and the rich fertile earth receives them to bear afresh.

I see the fireflies winking, hear the crickets and the locusts and the frogs. All are calling, calling, insistently, almost comically, "Here I am! Come. Come to me!"

"Male and female created he them," I think. For everything must have its opposite and meet with its opposite to be fulfilled.

Thank you, God, for this remarkable plan. Thank you for the hours of love it means.

I am as happy as one of those crickets singing in the grass.

I feel as tall and strong and lovely as one of those out-reaching trees. I feel as complete yet filled with promise as the earth teeming with its seeds.

Thank you, God, for making me a woman.

Fruit of Love

*No woman is ever so full of love as
when she is carrying a child.
Whether she planned the circumstance
or not she is trapped—literally locked
into a remarkable role: that of carrying
love. Man's love, her love, God's
love, all joined—united to fashion this
precious growing product: Life! Life, the
literal fruit of love.*

The Quarrel

God, we quarreled again last night, and today my heart is sore. My heart is heavy. It is literally heavy, as if a leaden weight were hanging in my breast.

And part of its weight is that he is bowed with it too. I keep seeing him, his head low, his shoulders actually bowed under it as he trudged off to work.

I can hardly bear the image. I could hardly bear it then. I wanted to run out and stop him, say nothing is worth this awful estrangement, say I'm sorry. But I didn't. I let him go, afraid more words might only lead to more quarreling.

I turned my sore heart back into this house, so heavily haunted by the quarrel. I drag myself about my tasks here, trying to forget the things we said.

But the words keep battering away at my sore heart and aching head. However I try to turn them off, they repeat themselves incessantly, a kind of idiot re-enactment of a play so awful that you keep trying to run out of the theater. Only all the exits are locked. The play goes on and on—and the worst of it is I keep adding more lines to it, trying to improve my part in it, adding things I wish I'd said.

God of love, please let this play end! Open the exits of my mind. Let the blessed daylight of forgiveness and forgetting pour in.

Bless him wherever he is. Lift the weight of this quarrel from his heart, his shoulders. I claim peace for him now, this minute. I claim and confirm your peace and joy for both of us when he returns.

"What Became of the Girl I Married?"

LOST: *One gay, sweet bride. Girl who thinks I'm wonderful and tells me so. Chief characteristic: Appreciation! Ample reward offered by one discouraged guy.*

Countless husbands could have composed that ad.

In the main, we women do a good job on our homes, our children, our community undertakings, and making ends meet. We don't come off too badly on the score of personal appearance, and most of us love our mates with depth and loyalty and passion. But far too many of us fall flat on our faces when it comes to showing those mates any real understanding or appreciation.

We fail in the first place, I believe, because we were not realistically prepared for marriage. Most of us floated down the aisle believing that our particular orange blossoms would never fade. Many a wife, instead of accepting her quite human but often quite wonderful husband for what he is, remains stubbornly in love with the prince of the fairy tales. And she will shove, shame, nag, weep, plead, and connive to try to fit her bewildered partner into the princely mold. That she knows it's impossible is beside the point. For she has also fallen in love with another deadly mirage: her own sense of having been wronged.

The woman who has formed the habit of thinking herself neglected is reluctant to relinquish the role even when she can! The very invitation she has been clamoring for, a date to go dancing or out on the town, is rejected: "You know I haven't anything decent to wear." (To come right down to it, she'd rather stay home than give up that precious: "You never take me anywhere.")

More women would find their longings fulfilled if they realized that romance is a two-way street. The wife who sits dourly at one end of it expecting love to come to her had better be prepared to sit a long time! But she who is willing to hop down from her high horse and come running halfway (and a little more) will find all her marriage relationships enriched.

For men like attention too. There are almost no men who do not feel a responsive leap when they are praised by their wives, told: "You're wonderful; I'm proud of you; I'm glad you're mine."

Before complaining too loudly of neglect, women should ask themselves honestly—who has the best of it? We may bear the children and rear them. We may wash, iron, clean, cook, quickfreeze, sew. But most of us have conveniences to make the going easier. And no law says we have to do these things.

A man, on the other hand, becomes an economic slave the minute he signs the marriage license. He is linked forever not only to the girl of his dreams but to his desk, or whatever means he has for her support. Because support her he must—and likewise any children she bears him. Morally and legally, he alone is responsible, and little short of death itself will ever free him. For even in case of separation or divorce this burden continues.

Just as a woman is under constant advertising pressure to be "alluring," a man gets constant financial pressure. He is attacked in his most vulnerable spot—his wife and kids. Take them vacationing in this roomier car; make them cooler with air conditioning, safer with fencing. And the most potent pleas come from the family itself: "The Beckers have bought a summer place, *why can't we?*"

Small wonder that so many men bury themselves in the financial pages, instead of whispering sweet nothings to their wives.

It may be true that husbands too often take love for granted, but women too often take for granted the responsibilities men assume for them. Ask any widow who is suddenly faced with the need to carry on alone. "When you have a good husband, you just don't realize how much he does," she will tell you. "Not until you're actually in his shoes can you appreciate what he's been up against. Then it's too late."

But for most of us it's not too late. Thank your husband for taking such good care of you—starting now. Praise him to his folks, his friends, and his offspring. Be grateful for his every little kindness—and show it!

If you are one of those who have been in love with your own misery, there is a good way to end the affair: Write yourself a letter. Turn a searchlight on your own faults, and list them honestly. Then set down every lovable trait, accomplishment, and quality of the man you married. You'll find such positive action a revelation in values, and you'll rise from it a far more appreciative, hence *lovable* wife.

Understanding and appreciation. The woman who can rediscover those virtues won't have to worry about romance. She'll have her share of it, and something even better—a guy who'll be saying, in his heart:

"FOUND: *the girl I married.*"

The Tender Trap

Oh, Lord, I'm so tired and lonely and blue I'm a little afraid. I'm so sick of housework, sick of the children. They get on my nerves so I could scream (and do). I'm even sick of my husband right now—I wish he'd go away on a trip.

Or I wish *I* could get away for a change. My husband says okay, go; go visit my sister. But that's not it. Even if I managed to leave the children I'd be around hers. . . . No, I want something else that has nothing to do with women and children. I want to be somebody else for a while. Maybe the girl I used to be, or maybe a woman I haven't even met yet. A beautiful, poised woman with a mind and life of her own.

Only I can't. There's never any going back to what you used to be. And right now there is no going ahead. There is only the present which sometimes seems such a trap. As the play called it—*The Tender Trap*. Only it was funny in the play, and it was the man who felt trapped.

Maybe my husband feels trapped too, going day after day to the same job. Maybe the people he has to deal with get on his nerves too (only a man can't scream). . . . And the women who leave their houses and fight traffic or crowded buses to get to work every day. Maybe they're screaming, too, somewhere inside.

Lord, help me to realize how lucky I am here, right now, within this tender trap. Turn my fantasies of escape to some purpose. If there's a woman I haven't met yet, locked somewhere inside me, let her out.

Bless that person you surely meant me to be, instead of this self-pitying drudge. Recreate me in her image. Help me to see that she is not some superior creature that would evolve out of other circumstances, but that she lives inside me.

Lord, I now affirm and claim her. I claim her poise, her calm, her patience, her cheerfulness, her self-control. I claim her beauty. I claim her awakened mind.

I claim her for my children. She will be a better mother.

I claim her for my husband. She will be a better wife.

I claim her for all women who are feeling the confines of their tender traps. Bless them and help each of them to find her too.

When a Husband Loses Interest

My husband has lost interest in me, Lord. I feel it. I know it.

I am less to him than his easy chair. Less to him than his dinner. Less than the TV set or his friends or his hobby or his newspaper.

At least such things comfort him or give him enjoyment. But me—it is as if I am invisible to him. He does not see me. He scarcely ever touches me. Even at night he has no need of me; he is asleep before I get to bed.

Lord, where have I failed that he takes me so for granted? Is his blindness and indifference perhaps a reflection of my own blindness and indifference to myself?

If I am no longer physically attractive, let me improve. Give me the time, energy, imagination, yes and the money, to become more appealing.

If I have become dull and boring, wake me, shake me, let me read more, think more, do more to be a better companion.

If I have nagged or scolded or complained without realizing it, show me these faults clearly, help me to change.

Dear Lord, please awaken my husband to my presence once again. Make him see me, touch me, know me, love me as a woman once more. With your help I can become someone more worth seeing, touching, knowing, loving.

Thank you for revealing this better self.

For Being Cherished

Lord, thank you for this simple yet priceless thing: Being cherished. For that old-fashioned word in old-fashioned wedding ceremonies, a word we take so for granted. Yet in reality how beautiful it is.

I'm untidy, my hair's a mess and so is the house. But the littlest fervently hugs my middle, and an eight-year-old presents me with a fragrant necklace of braided clover . . . A daughter banging in from school exclaims, "Hooray for anybody who can make gingerbread smell like that!" and gives me a kiss . . . My husband, toiling wearily in, perks up at sight of me and gives me another.

And suddenly, in a burst of awareness, I am overcome with this shining wonder: I am cherished!

I'm sick. Dizzy without warning. Trembling, not only with fatigue but a chill. Somebody says, "Go lie down, I'll finish the kitchen." I am being steered toward a hot bath, an already turned down bed. Cool hands are on my head.

I hear them making the phone calls I should be making, attending to things, sense their anxious tiptoeing about. And as I drift off there is something deeply sweet about even the misery that set all this in motion: I realize I am cherished.

We'll be late for the reception. As usual there's the last-minute search for the mislaid address; as usual I can't find my bag. And halfway down the block I set up a wail—a runner!

Patiently my husband turns back, waits with the motor running while I rush inside to change . . . And when I return, breathless, he leans over to pat my knee and say, "You're a lot of trouble, honey, but I guess you're worth it." And my heart leaps up in a little prayer of gratitude, God (I hope you hear it) just to thank you for being cherished.

When a Man Is Away

How many noises there are in a house when a man is gone!

Tickings and tappings and mysterious creakings. Slight rattlings and rumblings and thumpings heard at no other time . . . Maybe doors opening? . . . Footsteps approaching? Only don't be silly, don't be scared, everything's locked up tight . . . relax and go to SLEEP.

But the house refuses to be quiet. And the very night beyond its doors seems to want to come in. Branches scrape windows, leaves scurry across the steps, the wind fingers the shutters like a nosy woman shopping, and the rain whispers "Please."

Then the rain begins to rap, knock with a bold insistence. And though you smile and snuggle down, thinking, "Goody, I'm safe. Burglars and suchlike surely don't work much in the rain," yet the house seems to stir with new interest.

The cat begins to prowl, bell tinkling, but refuses to go out when you get up—not in the rain. Refuses even to cuddle down cozily at your feet . . . The dog begins to snore—great guttural blasts that almost drown out the cacophony of other noises (some protection SHE is!).

Since sleep seems to be hopeless, you turn on a lamp, make a cup of cocoa, and sip and read (something very soothing) until you're just too drowsy to hear them any more—these orchestras of night that seem to tune up only when there's no man in the house.

The Good Days of Marriage

Dear Lord, thank you for the good days of marriage. The days when we wake up pleased with each other, our jobs, our children, our home, and ourselves.

Thank you for our communication—the times when we can really talk to each other; and the times when we understand each other without so much as a gesture or a word.

Thank you for our companionship—the times when we can work together at projects we both enjoy. Or work in our separate fields and yet have that sense of sharing that can only come when two persons' lives have merged in so many other ways so long. Thank you that we don't feel cut off from each other, no matter how divergent the things we do.

Thank you for our times of privacy. Our times of freedom. Our relaxed sense of personal trust. Thank you that we don't have to clutch and stifle each other, that we have learned to respect ourselves enough to respect the other's individuality.

Thank you, Lord, that despite the many storms of marriage we have reached these particular shores. Help us to remember them. Help us to hold fast to them, Lord.

Family
   Love

For a Wanted Child

Oh, God, thank you for the child I carry.

I am in love with it as I am in love with my husband and my life—and you.

I walk the world in wonder. I see it through new eyes.

All is changed, subtly but singingly different. The beauty of sunlight upon the grass, the feel of its warmth along my arms. It is cradling me in tenderness as I shall cradle this child one day.

I am mother and child in one, new as a child myself, innocent, excited, amused, surprised.

I marvel at my changing body. It is as sweet and new to me as when I was a little girl. Even its symptoms are less of misery or fatigue than signals of its secret. "See how important I am," my body claims. "Feel my insistence as I make and shape this child for you."

God, I am happy. God, I am sad. God, I am vital—alive, alive. Life has me in its hands. Life is moving me in an immutable direction that I don't want to resist and couldn't if I tried.

It is almost comical, this sweet and stern insistence. It is like night and day and the changing of the seasons. "Stop, stop!" I might as well cry to the winds or the sea.

No, no, I am in for it now, and I rejoice, though I am also a little bit afraid. The labor, the delivery, the care. But it is an exciting kind of anxiety. It is part of the privilege of being female.

Oh, God, bless this body in which the mystery of life is working. Let it be equal to its job.

And bless the tiny marvel it is responsible for. Your handiwork! Oh, bless my baby too—let it be whole and beautiful and strong.

A Prayer for Fathers

God bless fathers, all fathers old and young.

Bless the new father holding his son or daughter in his arms for the first time. (Steady his trembling, Lord, make his arms strong.)

Give him the ambition and strength to provide for its physical needs. But even more, give him the love and common sense to provide for its hungering heart.

Give him the time and the will to be its friend. Give him wisdom, give him patience, give him justice in discipline.

Make him a hero in his youngster's eyes. So that the word Father will always mean a person to be respected, a fair and mighty man.

And God bless older fathers too.

Fathers who are weary from working for their young. Fathers who are sometimes disappointed, discouraged. Fathers whose children don't always turn out the way they'd hoped; fathers of children who seem thoughtless, ungrateful, critical, children who rebel.

Bless those fathers, Lord; comfort them.

And stay close to all these fathers when they must tell sons and daughters good-bye. When kids leave home, going off to college, or to marry, or to war—fathers need to be steadied in their trembling then too, Lord. (Mothers aren't the only ones who cry.)

You, our heavenly father, must surely understand these earthly fathers well.

We so often disappoint you, rebel against you, fail to thank you, turn away from you. So, in your infinite love (and infinite experience!) bless fathers, all fathers old and young.

Bathtime

No matter how busy I am, Lord, let me be thankful and find joy in bathing my baby—he's growing so fast. No longer tiny and helpless, almost lost in a long white nightie, but now full to my arms, with a rollicking will of his own.

Thank you for the sight of his back straight and sturdy in the tub, and the perfect peach globe of his head. (Please keep him always straight and strong.) For the sheer bright abandon of his antics—his mad splashing, his impassioned clutch of floating ship and ball. For the foolishness of a chewed washcloth dribbling daily down his chin, and the flirtatious peeking of his eyes over the tub's rim.

My son, Lord, my plump brazen elf of a son to be soaped and rinsed as he scolds and sings and chatters in his own expressive jargon. My son to be gathered warm and wet into a big towel, to be patted and powdered and oiled.

I lift him up in a joyous little gesture of offering, and he dances on tiptoe with nimble nakedness.

Thank you for this son to be wrestled into a diaper. For he keeps flopping over, scrambling to his knees—it is like trying to put pants on the wind! Yet you made mothers strong-fingered and determined. We must win the kicking contest against shoes and stockings, we must subdue our offspring into clothes.

And our reward is to carry a son at last, sweet and fresh, clasping our neck, riding royally down to his dinner like a king.

Thank you for this child and this happy daily struggle that is half duty, half delight. And whenever it seems a chore, help me to remember how awfully fast little boys get too big to be bathed . . . or maneuvered into *any*thing.

A Son

A son is surely the most remarkable thing that can happen to a man and wife.

A man usually wants a boy first, to be sure of carrying on the family name. Men need this firm symbolic title to the past. They want it spelled out, printed, inscribed on documents, carved in stone. They don't want the chain broken. It is their lifeline.

A woman doesn't need this reassurance. She takes her measure of immortality with every child she bears. Yet it pleases her to think—some day their son will bestow this proud name upon his wife! Like herself and John, *they* will be the Smiths, the Andersons.

But long before this can happen, the subject has to be taught, trained, hauled places, exhorted to study and to practice, conferred about with teachers, coaches, Scout leaders and the neighbors. In his behalf there are innumerable meetings to endure, programs to applaud, dinners to down. His tonsils must usually be deleted, his teeth fixed, his feet fitted into an appalling parade of ever bigger more expensive shoes. Even shoes run second, however, to the incredible number of pants that a boy is able to ruin, outgrow, or even lose.

There is all his equipment to be procured. His ball bats, camping gear, football helmets, fishing tackle, swim trunks and track shoes.

And his means of propulsion! Today's boy takes to wheels as soon as he can straddle a tricycle, and is seldom separated from them until he takes off in a jet plane or a rocket to the moon. Between these points the parents spend enough time in arguments, discussion, trips to the doctor, the insurance agent, and sometimes the police station (not to mention the hours of lying awake worrying) to have personally paved at least ten miles of local highway, or written most of Shakespeare's plays.

As for the pets and projects . . . The escaping hamsters, the injured birds and wormy squirrels, the dead butterflies, the cats, dogs, rabbits, snakes, racoons—and eventually, girls . . . The courses in hypnotism and taxidermy; the hikes and hideouts and tents and secret clubs. The stamp and coin collections, the chemistry experiments.

A mother's reward for all this is the thrill of finally discovering a compound that will take the stains out of the sofa, and the relief of being told at the hospital that he didn't get his neck broken falling out of the tree house. If you're lucky (and strong-willed) you also have someone to carry out the trash, run errands, and (police brutality) rake and mow the yard.

Less definite but dear returns are: A snaggle-toothed grin from a school bus . . . A limp bunch of violets . . . An unexpected hug . . . The shout, "I got an A!" or "I made the team!" . . . A neighbor's remark: "He's the best paper boy we've ever had." . . . A trumpet's stubborn tooting . . . A football game where he makes the winning touchdown (or they at least call him in to substitute). . . . The look of a thin neck and tender young shoulders going off in a white jacket with a corsage box under the arm . . . A voice sweeter than all others in the choir . . .

Finally he gets his diploma (where's yours?) and sometimes follows in his father's footsteps, but more often goes striding off on paths of his own. Sometimes he falls by the wayside and doesn't seem to be going anyplace. And these are times that try parental souls. But eventually (if you just live long enough) he picks himself up and rushes forward toward achievements beyond your fondest dreams.

A son may worry you, disappoint you, keep you broke. Or he may excel, fulfill every ambition, make you so proud you think you'll explode. Anyway, he leaves a cluttered trail on his way to manhood—schoolbooks, papers, marbles, fish hooks, tennis racquets, souvenirs, and autographed pictures. He abandons a lot of gear, outgrows a lot of trousers, and wears out a lot of shoes. But he will always carry your hope in his hip pocket, and he can never lose or wear out your faith in him, or your love.

He's stuck with it. It's his heritage, his lifeline—as permanent as his father's family name.

I Was So Cross to the Children

Oh, God, I was so cross to the children today. Forgive me.

Oh, God, I was so discouraged, so tired, and so unreasonable. I took it out on them. Forgive me.

Forgive me my bad temper, my impatience, and most of all my yelling.

I cringe to think of it. My heart aches. I want to go down on my knees beside each little bed and wake them up and beg them to forgive me. Only I can't, it would only upset them more.

I've got to go on living with the memory of this day. My unjust tirades. The guilty fear in their eyes as they flew about trying to appease me. Thinking it all their fault—*my* troubles, my disappointments.

Dear God, the utter helplessness of children. Their vulnerability before this awful thing, adult power. And how forgiving they are, hugging me so fervently at bedtime, kissing me good night.

And all I can do now is to straighten a cover, move a toy fallen out of an upthrust hand, touch a small head burrowed into a pillow, and beg in my heart, "Forgive me."

Lord, in failing these little ones whom you've put into my keeping, I'm failing you. Please let your infinite patience and goodness fill me tomorrow. Stand by me, keep your hand on my shoulder. Don't let me be so cross to my children.

Little Boys

Your little boy awakes and cries because of a bad dream.

His hot small body clings to you as you sit on the edge of the bed. You feel the firm curves of it through the thin crumpled pajamas. His fat cheeks are moist and the tips of his lashes are moist and fragile, too, against your cheek.

You hold him on your lap and comfort him and know the joy of holding and comforting him, of being his mother to whom he turns when unhappy or afraid.

You think of some fracas in the yard, his demanding in a plaintive howl, "Mummy, help! Billy took my shubble!" And though he is sent back usually to settle the trouble himself, it comes to you with some thrilling sense of wonder and privilege how good it is to be, for this little while, supreme commander of his day. The person omnipotent, who is empowered and entrusted to heal all hurts, answer all questions, meet all his many demands.

And holding and comforting him there in the dark, you think how soon he will be a big leggy boy, remote and roughly shy, not wanting your caresses any more.

And how he will become a man and go away from home and perhaps do splendid things, things of which you'll boast, but in which life gives no mother any real part. How you will become a shadowy figure to him, someone of whom he thinks with fondness and tenderness and concern, perhaps, but no longer vital or essential to him, because that is life's way.

And it comes to you how brief and filled with glory are these early years of parenthood.

How those who are young mothers are creatures of special privilege, for all the trouble and bother and often unutterable weariness we know. How we should live every moment with our youngsters to the utmost, creating bright memories and hoarding them like riches against the inevitable loss to come.

Few, so tragically few of us, have the faintest conception of what other, older women feel.

"This is my son!" they proudly say, taking a photograph from the mantel and speaking of his accomplishments, while we murmur polite admiration.

This night, however, holding your own little fellow, you begin to understand:

He is lost to them. Gone. But in showing his picture to others, speaking of him to people who can't possibly care, they are recreating him for themselves. Bringing back the little boy who woke up crying in the night, who could be comforted, caressed, and held close against his too swift growing up.

A Child's Hand in Yours

What feeling in all the world is so nice as that of a child's hand in yours?

It is soft. It is small and warm. It is as innocent and guileless as a rabbit or a puppy or a kitten huddling in the shelter of your clasp. Or it is like living clay to be molded. It is the essence of all trust.

"Here I am," it seems to tell you. "Shape me. Guide me. Lead me."

If you stop to consider, the responsibility it imposes is almost too much. But you don't. "Here, take my hand while we're crossing the street," you say, and concentrate on the immediate business of getting him safely to the curb. Or, "Hold onto my hand, Mother will see that the dog doesn't bite you, don't be afraid."

Or you take the feverish, betrayed little fingers in yours after the tonsils are out and say, "I know it hurts, darling, but it won't last long. Just hang onto my hand until you fall asleep."

A child's hand in yours—what tenderness it arouses, what almost formidable power it conjures up! You are instantly not only the symbol but the very touchstone of security, wisdom, and strength.

Though you may secretly know yourself to be lacking in all these things, miraculously the child endows you with them as he reaches up. As he clutches your own hand so unquestioningly, he is giving back the very qualities that he draws from that hand to comfort himself.

He is making you taller and stronger and wiser. He is leading you just a little nearer to the person he imagines you to be.

And a child's hand in yours is something more. It is your link with life itself. For each son or daughter is a projection of those who created him.

A mother clasping her little girl's hand, a father gripping the fingers of his small son—each is leading his own dreams forward, holding fast to his own tomorrows.

A Tent

Children must all be the descendants of nomads, for they would live their lives out, if you let them, in a tent.

They discover the joy of this triangular shelter when they are very young. Let any mother start airing blankets on a line, and her offspring are sure to come scurrying between the blankets' flapping sides.

"A tent! A tent!" they shout in delight. "This will be my tent and that pink one yours. We'll be neighbors and live in our tents."

Sometimes they prevail on their mother to string up a line especially for the purpose and over it drape an old unused spread or quilt. Staked to the ground with little sticks, it makes a lovely tent. There, with their dolls and their dishes and their little toy stoves, they set up housekeeping, crawling joyfully in and out to obtain crackers and jelly sandwiches and to pick tiny bouquets of clover or dandelions. They urge you to creep in on all fours—into this cozy, sun-fragrant, grassy haven, where they crouch in such delight.

When they are older, they must have a real canvas tent to make their pleasure complete. A waterproof tent, where they can be snug even in a shower. A place where they can sometimes "sleep out." A tent to take on camping trips. Every summer, their dad digs it out from under the porch and aids in setting it up in the yard.

And there, for a few days, it becomes the social center of the neighborhood. Club meetings are held there, and tea parties, and fights. And the inevitable pleas bombard you: "Oh, please, may we sleep out tonight? Let us sleep in the tent!"

This, too, usually brings on arguments. The little ones want to join the big ones and their friends, which is unthinkable: "We want to *talk!* Besides there isn't room." The boys want it the same night as the girls. "And don't forget whose tent it really is," some long-forgotten claim is laid. "I got it for Scouts, remember. So it's *my tent!*"

And when some of these matters are settled, the most elaborate plans go oft awry. Mosquitoes, a hoot owl, an unexpected fright ("We heard this *terrible noise!*") will send a covey of girls tearing to the house, clutching their sheets. And even when they do finally settle down and get to sleep, *you* can't. They're so crowded, how do they stand it? And it's chilly. Have they got enough blankets? You toss and turn and worry and finally steal outside with a flashlight. Cautiously, you lift the flap and peer in.

And there, crammed together on the hard ground, they are blissfully snoozing. Close to nature, close to their primordial ancestors, no doubt, they are sleeping the sleep of the wild, the free, the innocent; the peaceful sleep of the young, when all the world is new and summertime is eternal—in a tent.

I Spanked My Child Today

I spanked my child today.
She'd torn her dress at play
And tracked across the rug
And peered at me in such a smug,
Defiant, impish way,
I sort of lost my head.
I spanked her till her little
Spanking place was red.
But now that she's in bed
I don't know what to say.
It's . . . . hard . . . .
A sleeping child
Is such a chokey sight,
The face so very small
Against the pillow white,
The hands upthrown,
A toy on guard,
The fair hair mussed . . . .
If I've betrayed
My sacred tiny trust,
Oh, Lord of little children,
Please forgive
And let me give
The scales of love
An extra disc of patience
To outweigh . . . .
I wish I hadn't
Spanked my child today.

I'm Tired of All the Experts

Listen, Lord . . .

I'm tired of all the experts.

People who try to tell me how to raise my children, how to run my marriage, how to be a better person, how to save the world.

I've listened to them far too often, been intimidated by them too often. I have underestimated my own instincts and common sense—and you.

I am going back to the Bible for some good old-fashioned guidance: "Honor thy father and thy mother." "Bring up a child in the way he should go and he will not depart from it." "Love thy neighbor as thyself."

Yes, and the Ten Commandments, and a whole lot more.

I'm going to rediscover this long neglected gold mine, God. I'm going to see how it stacks up against the advice of today's so-called experts.

(And while I'm at it, I'm going to be a lot more careful about posing as an expert myself.)

Little Girls Together

How delightful is the friendship that exists between little girls. Small females somewhere between the ages of six and ten.

When they are smaller they will quarrel over toys. They cry and get mad and go home. When they are older they compete. They will hurt each other's feelings. Many times they talk mercilessly about each other, even the closest chums. They can weep their hearts out on a pillow over a real or fancied snub.

But when they are first grade playmates, or second, or third or fourth, then they are still exactly that: Companions in play. In secrets. In giggling games. In merry undertakings which include everything from baking a package cake to selling cold drinks, or organizing a back yard show or a Witch's Club.

Their laughter is as sparkling and without malice as a bright morning shower. Their jokes are bold, obvious, usually old as the stars, and utterly without guile. They make up insane songs with which to accompany their rope jumpings, or the bouncing of a ball. They call each other up mornings and evenings to giggle, exchange lengthy lists of what they hope to get for their birthdays, and make vast impossible plans for building a playhouse or buying a horse.

Spending the night together is a thrilling undertaking which involves lugging along a bulging bag of stuffed animals as well as their best pajamas, robe, slippers, bubble bath, and at least one doll with complete wardrobe. They climb joyously from bed to bed, bounce, throw pillows, and keep each other awake with scary stories.

At last, after many remonstrances and warnings, they collapse into the profound sleep of childhood. Stealing in, you find them sprawled in incredible positions, legs dangling over the bedside, pigtails or curls awry, covers trailing the floor. They are usually awake at dawn, singing, cavorting, and buzzing like bees over their marvelous plans for the day.

Little girls playing together in this wonderful morning of their lifetime are like young birds chirping, or butterflies winging lightly among the flowers. They need each other in a way that is instinctive and joyous; they are nourished by each other's presence, they thrive and grow strong in the light of each other's warmth, as plants grow unconsciously upward in the light of the sun.

For an Unexpected Child

Dear God, it's true, we're going to have another child. And I am aghast, I am stunned. I didn't expect this, I didn't want it, and there's no use pretending—to you or to myself—I don't want it now.

With so many childless women longing for babies, why have you chosen me? You, who are the Author and Giver of Life, as the prayer book says—why not one of them? Why me, why me?

I don't need or want this gift. I am not grateful for it. I don't understand your ways.

"Some day it will be a great comfort to you," the doctor says. And some deep abiding instinct assures me he is right. But that is small comfort *now*.

Then there is that other cliché, "The Lord will provide." And you will, financially you will, you always have.

Yet I don't want to have to wait for that proof either. Provide for me *now*. Provide for this child. Provide me with love and joy and a feeling of welcome for this little new unexpected life.

The Nursery

There they lie, in their little glass garden, these fragile new fruits of human love. And of your love too, the eternal love that flows through the universe, creating and re-creating these exquisite creatures in your image.

There they sleep, God, in the blessed sleep of their newness. So fresh from the mystery of their beginning, so warm and moist and sweet from the waters in which they were cradled.

Resting from the rude shock of birth they lie. . . . Resting . . . resting for the long journey ahead.

Though one or two awake and start yelling—lustily, comically demanding the rescue that quickly comes. Hands, gently efficient, to change and feed and comfort them. To hold them up before the pleased eyes of the people gazing in.

There they sleep, God, or are displayed, wrapped in the most complete and absolute love they will ever know.

Then one grandmother, old and broken with living, smiles faintly and shakes her head. "Poor little things," she remarks as she turns away. "If they only knew what's ahead."

And my heart gives a little start of sorrow. I too am suddenly stricken. For I see these children rising and walking, stripped of protection, of warm blankets and sheltering arms.

I see some of them cold, frightened, struggling—against danger, violence, physical abuse, drugs. I see them tempted, I see them shaken. I see them bitter with heartbreak, confusion, despair. And my whole being cries out to you, "No, no, spare them, keep them here!"

But I know you wouldn't have it so. *They* wouldn't have it. They are as hungry for the life struggle as they are for milk. It is their right; they are savagely insistent upon it.

They sleep now . . . However sweetly they sleep now . . . they must rise up and go. But oh, Lord, when the blissful sleep is over and they take their first faltering steps, give us patience, give us wisdom. Show us how to help them.

For now, bless them as they lie resting for the journey ahead.

Night Duty

Oh, Lord, I hear it again, that little voice in the night, crying, "Mommy!"

At least I think I hear it. It may be my imagination. It may be just the wind. Or if not, maybe it will stop in a minute, the child will go back to sleep. . . .

(Oh, let it be just the wind. Or let him go back to sleep. I'm so tired. I've been up so many nights lately. I've got to get some sleep too.)

But if it's true, if it's one of them needing me and it isn't going to stop, if I must go—help me.

Lift me up, steady me on my feet. And make me equal to my duty.

If he's scared give me patience and compassion to drive the fears of night away.

If he's ill give me wisdom. Make me alert. Let me know what to do.

If he's wet the bed again, give me even more patience and wisdom and understanding (and let me find some clean sheets).

Thank you, Lord, for helping my weary footsteps down this hall.

Thank you for sustaining me too as I comfort and care for the child.

Thank you for my own sweet . . . sweet . . . eventual sleep.

Lucky Is the Woman
with Daughters

Lucky is the woman who has daughters.

They're so lovely when they're little, with their bonnets and bows. Fun to sew for, to bathe and cuddle, to dress. Boys resist much of this; whereas daughters whisk you back to your childhood. Daughters are your dolls. And daughters increase in value as they grow older, because there are so many things mothers and daughters can share.

A daughter is made in your image. As if to enhance this happy marvel we go through a phase of mother-daughter outfits (luckily, short-lived). But hard on its heel rides the wish to turn out a product which is pretty and popular, witty, wise and good. A kind of impossible package mix of all that we probably were NOT at her age. We watch the clock praying she'll have a good time at the party, and know an ancient heartbreak when she weeps, "It was awful, only one boy danced with me and he's a fink!" Or, when she rushes in starry-eyed, we waltz to a secret tune.

At about this time we discover the mixed blessings of mother-daughterdom. There is a continual pirating of perfume, nail polish, lipsticks, rollers, sweaters and hose. Which grows, with their acquisitions, into a kind of female mutual fund. "I never have anything I can call my own," a mother may lament, adding, "But I've doubled my potential supply of accessories and clothes."

Also, daughters come in handy once they've taken home economics. Now they can fit and fix some of your things, as well as their own. And there's nothing more satisfying, if rather touching, than to hear the sewing machine humming as a daughter sticks gamely to the cause of making her own prom dress.

By now it's no longer Mom who's passing on the tricks of glamor—it's the girls. They're suddenly so good at hair, they're doing yours. Also, helping you make up your eyes before a party, advising you which hat to wear and for Pete's sake to hold your stomach in. For scarcely have they put their toys away, it seems, than today's daughters become wonderfully wise in the feminine arts.

Alas, perhaps too wise! For daughters can be wildly exasperating to shop with. They detest everything you like, making you feel about as hip on fashion as The Girl of the Limberlost. But they're also fun to pause and have a snack with when you've almost come to blows.

Mad as little girls are about "helping Mother" scrub, iron, cook, by the time they're old enough to be some use around a house, they're usually off somewhere, or on the telephone. And their rooms are invariably a mess. Preoccupied with the lengthy rites of bedtime, and the preparations as if for a beauty pageant before taking off for school, they leave in their wake a welter of open drawers, horses, Beatles, stuffed animals, strewn garments, and unmade beds. I know of no cure for this except for the girl to join the Marines, go away to college, or get married. And when this happens you miss them so acutely you'd rather have the chaos.

Yet mothers and daughters occupy a secret country of the feminine where you can giggle, gossip, discuss your ailments, share your dreams. That's why misunderstandings between them are so painful, quarrels so devastating. And yet inevitable. For nature, at whatever cost to both of you, decrees that your bright, your beautiful, kind-cruel daughters must cast you aside, break free.

My own mother used to say: "A daughter is just her mother's heart walking around outside her." I know now what she meant.

A Mother's Prayer in the Morning

Thank you, Lord, for this glorious day.

Bless the carpet beneath my feet and the bombardment of hot and cold water that freshens my waking skin.

Bless the breakfast I am cooking for my family, and the special music of morning around me—doors banging, the clatter of forks and plates, the rattle of lunch boxes, children demanding "Mother!"

Thank you for my healthy available presence that is able to cope with them.

Bless the husband who provides all this. Be with him as he sets off for work; fill him with a sense of his own worth and achievement, enrich and enliven his day.

Bless the school buses and their drivers, let them transport our children safely.

Bless the teachers and that marvelous institution that claims my offspring for the next important hours. Please let them be good there, happy there, bright and able to grasp the lessons there, and oh, thank you that they're well enough to *be* there.

Now bless this quiet house—even its confusion and disorder which speaks so vividly of its quality of life. Thank you that I have the time and the strength to straighten it.

And thank you for the freedom to sit down with a cup of coffee before I begin!

For a Child Adventuring

At two:
Into the perilous world you'd trot,
With never a backward look.
Into the teeming traffic,
Into the rushing brook.
"Come back!" I cry, and snatch you,
Small bird, against my breast,
To cuddle and caress you
And keep you safe in your nest.

At twenty:
Into the dazzling world you stride
With scarcely a backward glance,
Into the cruel, competitive race—
Into romance.
"Come back!" cries my heart.
   "There's danger."
Knowing it does no good,
Knowing I'd never dim your dreams
Nor keep you if I could.

Let Them Remember Laughter

Lord, whatever else my family remembers of me (the mistakes, the tears, the temper) please let them also remember my laughter. Guard me against ever becoming a grim and cheerless mother unable to see the funny side, even when things go wrong.

Lord, keep my laughter especially on tap when I'm the culprit in the case: When I've locked us all out of the house or the car . . . When my lovingly molded mousse skids onto the kitchen floor . . . When I've pulled some awful boo-boo with the president of the P.T.A. or the grande dame of the neighborhood . . . When I've dyed my hair the wrong color, or ruined a dress I was making, or gotten us all hopelessly entangled in wet wallpaper . . . help me to see the comedy of my errors.

Instead of stamping and storming, let me give my children the healing gift of laughter.

Lord, let me be a mother who can laugh with her children.

Don't let me ever laugh *at* them when they're trying to please me, no. Never when they're awkward, discouraged or troubled. But remind me to laugh more freely, gaily at their antics and their stories. Yea, though I've witnessed such clowning so often, heard the same jokes before, equip me with patience and a convincing show of enthusiasm. They need an audience so much.

Let me applaud with my heart as well as my hands. Help me to give them the sweet gift of laughter.

The same thing goes for my husband, God.

He needs an audience too, he needs a cheering section (and goodness knows after all these years *his* comedy routines are familiar). But mainly let him remember me as laughing more often than crying the blues.

I know that a family means problems, Lord. A family means troubles large and small. Troubles I can't always expect to "come smiling through." But with your help no troubles can overcome us, and laughter helps too.

Lord, let no day pass that my family doesn't hear my laughter.

Good Roots

Help me to give my children good roots, God.

As I work with my plants I can see that the sturdiest, and those which bear most freely, are those whose roots go deep, gripping rich soil; they have a base from which they can grow tall and beautiful and sound.

Let this household furnish that kind of soil for my family, God. Enriched with good music, good books, good talk, good taste. But above all, goodness of spirit. Goodness of action.

So that those who come here feel welcome, and those who leave here feel warm. And those who live here know, in every fiber of their beings, that they belong to people who, for all our faults, are good people. People of decency and honor, who would not willingly hurt or cheat any living thing.

Let my children grow freely, God, in whatever direction their nature directs. But give them root strength, too. So that they will never deviate too far from their own beginnings.

Help me to give my children good roots.

Her Ark and Her Covenant

It has been said of man that his home is his castle. But what of woman? Strangely, few phrases have been coined to express the significance of home to her, the person who presides over its every function. What, then, is home to a woman?

Often, to be quite honest, home represents chaos, confusion, and quarrels. It is a place so hectic that sometimes, if we are human, we long only to escape. Time and again women, good women, have said to me, "I reach a point where I actually have insane thoughts of running off. Just any place to get away!"

A great deal of the time home to a woman is just plain old-fashioned work. Meals and dishes and ironing curtains and cleaning the closets and washing clothes.

Frequently it is entertaining. Everything slick and shining, and heavenly smells from the oven, and counting the silver, and baths early for everybody so that fresh towels can be up. And flowers and mints and nuts, and the sheer delight of pleasant voices exclaiming, "My, what a beautiful home."

A lot of the time it's worry—four walls that hold more concentrated concern than it seems any soul can bear: Will your son pass? Is your daughter really serious about that impossible boy she insists on seeing? Why can't the doctors find out what's wrong with John? Why doesn't money go further? How will the budget stand the added strain of college?

A great deal of the time it's fun. Small fry prancing about, so comically sweet in their antics you must scoop them into your arms. Teen-agers doing card tricks, dancing, playing the piano. Neighbors popping in for coffee. Your husband cornering you in the kitchen to tell you that funny story he heard at his luncheon club.

Her home is all these things to a woman, and a whole lot more. Something intangible. Something deeper. Something impossible to capture in a phrase.

Home is both the place where she is sheltered from the world, yet where her weaknesses and failures are exposed. Both the prison from which she cannot escape, yet the place where she is freest.

And here, for all its turbulence and burdens, she is its keynote. The touchstone for other people's progress. The focal point from which the spokes of their lives radiate.

As such, her home is not a matter of rugs and linens and beds and the washing machine and the kitchen stove. It is not the walls that surround it nor the contents of its rooms. It is both an ark—and a covenant.

Her ark for her protection. Her covenant with the future. It is her destiny.

Daughter, Daughter

How straight she sleeps, how slender-tall,
Daughter, daughter, recent small.
Gone the braids and pinafores
And paper dolls across the floors.
Party clothes across the bed,
Her hair spills shining free instead.
An orchid floats within the dish
That once held turtle, snail and fish.
Gone the tomboy, gone the child,
A woman dreams here, life-beguiled.

The bough must break, the bud must flower.
Daughter, daughter, soon the hour
When you, like others, come to wife.
This the pattern, this—life.
But let me stand one moment brief
Cupping again the uncurled leaf
So small, so safe upon the tree—
Daughter, daughter, close to me.

Hold Me Up a Little Longer

Hold me up a little longer, Lord, just a little longer.

I've been up since before daylight and it's so late and this P.T.A. speaker drones on and on. Just keep me awake until he stops (please make it soon) and revive me enough to help serve the doughnuts and coffee and get home.

The miles I've put on the car stretch behind me like a trip through eternity instead of a single day. To market and music lessons and the vet's. To the laundromat after our machine broke down. To the doctor's after our son got hit with a base-ball bat. (Thank you, oh thank you that it wasn't serious, after all.)

What else, Lord? I'm too tired to remember. I just know that off somewhere there's a hot bath waiting. A bed waiting . . . my own dear sweet bed is waiting and the time will actu-ally arrive when I'll sink gratefully into it . . . It will even be morning . . . tomorrow . . . next week!

Thank you for this image of respite, Lord. Of rest and en-ergy renewed. Right now, this minute, prop me up, revive me.

Hang onto me just a little longer, Lord.

Paper Boy

Oh, Lord, his alarm's gone off, I can hear it ringing . . . ringing . . . as I lie here so snugly in bed. Please let him hear it and get up without having to be called. (Maybe if I just slipped in, without waking his father . . .)

There now, thank you, he's stirring, it's stopped, he's dressing. (Please let him put on a warm shirt and his boots instead of sneakers, it's so cold, it's snowing.)

Now his door is opening, I can hear him clumping downstairs (thank you, Lord, that he's wearing his boots). Please help him to find his heavy gloves (they're right there on the hall table) and please, please make him wear something on his head for a change, that wind is fierce. (Maybe I should get up and help him find it. Or try and persuade him . . . And fix him some breakfast, only he'd probably have a fit.)

Now he's getting his bike from the driveway. (I can't help it, Lord, I just had to come to the window to watch—and sure enough his head is bare, and the bike's all covered with snow, he's got to brush it off . . . Why, *why* won't he put it in the garage like he's been told?)

Lord, help him, please help him as he lugs the heavy bundle from the corner where it's been tossed. And the wind's blowing so hard, help him as he stuffs the papers into his bag and struggles the whole thing onto his shoulder. (Maybe I should throw on a coat and run down to give him a hand . . . Maybe I should even go with him.)

Should I, Lord? Tell me, help me . . . only it's too late anyway now. There he goes wobbling off down the snowy street. I might as well crawl back into my own warm bed . . . But, oh Lord, keep him safe. Don't let him get too cold or make too many mistakes this morning, and please get him back in time for a good hot breakfast before Sunday School.

And now, Lord, forgive me all this worrying. Let me go back to sleep knowing you will protect him, you are with him, you will put your loving arms around him.

Thank you that he wanted this job and for the lessons he's learning. Thank you, Lord, for my son and his paper route.

"Supper's Ready!"

Whatever happened to the family dinner hour? Or "supper" as we called it in our small town? That time at the end of the day when everybody was summoned to wash up and sit down together to share a common meal. A time not only to eat but to talk to each other, even if you sometimes quarreled. A time and place where you could laugh, joke, exchange ideas, tell stories, dump your troubles. (Yes, and learn your manners.)

Surely its disappearance has a lot to do with the much lamented disintegration of the American family. We've traded it in on the TV set and a freezer stuffed with prepack foods. We've exchanged it gaily for the cocktail hour. We've let it get lost in the flurry of meetings, lessons, parties, and activities to which we have mortgaged our evenings today. None of these things are particularly harmful in themselves, most in fact are essentially progressive and pleasant. But nonetheless an insidious encroachment and ultimately the destroyer of a daily custom that could not but contribute to family solidarity.

"Suppertime!" The last meal of the day . . .

Only city folks or people who put on city airs called it dinner. To us dinner was at noon, and we didn't mean lunch, we meant *dinner*. When we spoke of three square meals a day we meant three square meals. During the morning, along with everything else she had to do, a woman was also getting dinner. Tending the pot roast or pounding the beefsteak, cooking the vegetables and potatoes, making a custard and opening a Mason jar of pears or home-canned applesauce. And promptly on the stroke of twelve it had to be ready. For at that point the town's activities would come to a sudden halt with the blasting of the noon whistle at the firehouse.

On that instant stores and offices closed, school got out. A few doctors and lawyers and businessmen ate at Martin's Cafe or the Bradford Hotel, but most men headed for home. Since we had no school cafeterias or buses we walked home too—only the country kids, whom we envied, were allowed to bring their lunches. Winter or spring, fair weather or foul, we walked; and since our house was more than a mile away, it was stow away all that food and start back so you wouldn't be late. (To be tardy was a disgrace.) Anyway, noon dinner in our town was an hour of suspended activity, except for a sense of clicking dishes and earnestly munching jaws.

Supper was different. More leisurely. Less a time of common refueling than an hour when everybody gathered at the day's end to summarize and share what had gone on. And it varied with families. You'd begin to hear the calls, "Hey, kids, come on now, time to help get supper—" or the announcement, "Supper's ready!" all over the neighborhood anywhere from five o'clock on. People like the Renshaws ate early; Mr. Renshaw worked the night shift at the creamery and liked a long evening with his family before he donned his white overalls and departed. Judge J. Rutherford Jensen was to be seen stalking up the steps between the white Corinthian columns of his house at 5:15, expecting his food to be on the table and his children ready to sit down. Mrs. Flanders who liked to gad and was sort of slapdash about her cooking never managed to round up her brood until nearly seven o'clock—to the horror of some women and the distress of many kids, because most of us had finished the dishes by then and were ready to play out again.

But whether you ate at five or six or seven, one thing we had in common: Everybody had to *be* there. And in most households everybody had to help.

We thought the boys got off easy after we'd converted to cooking with gas. Before that they'd had to chop the kindling for the range, carry in the baskets of mealy red cobs, and from dusky bins in the basement haul up the snout-mouthed coal buckets. Theirs too the duty of trimming the wicks on the oilstove, cleaning its yellowed isinglass chimneys, and filling its tank with kerosene poured from a can with a potato stuck on its spout. Since Mother didn't quite trust her gas stove, especially for baking, they still sometimes had to. And after supper they had to carry out the scraps.

Even very little girls were summoned in to put the teakettle on and start the potatoes. Potatoes were as essential to supper as the silverware. Boiled potatoes or fried; for company scalloped or mashed; but inevitably potatoes. And since you'd usually had them boiled for dinner and there were generally plenty left over, the cold, boiled globes were chopped up, salted, peppered, and fried.

Mother was not an impassioned cook. She felt a defensive, half-guilty distress for women who spent most of their time in the kitchen. "All that work just for something to put in your mouth and swallow, just to fill your stomach, just to *eat*." To her, food for the soul was just as important, and she feasted richly, if indiscriminately, on Tennyson and Tarkington, Shakespeare and Grace Noll Crowel and Harold Bell Wright. A true "book drunk," as she described herself, she would often become so absorbed that it would be late afternoon before she came to, shocked to discover from the redolent odors wafting up and down the block that other people's suppers were cooking. "Oh, dear, what'll we have?" she would worry vaguely, and start summoning offspring for calculations and tasks.

If in summer, someone would be dispatched to pick, pull, or dig whatever was ready from the garden, and fingers would fly, snapping, shelling, or peeling things. Meanwhile, tapping her gold tooth, she would achieve a small list of items for when the phone would ring and whoever was downtown would ask, "What do you want for supper?" Often she dismissed the whole business with a cheerful, "Oh, I don't care, just whatever looks good."

Dad didn't mind and he bought with a lavish hand when he

could. If times were plentiful the meat was invariably thick red beefsteak, and the sack would be full of surprises like Nabiscos and coconut-topped marshmallow cookies, along with cherry pie from the bakery, and white grapes. And maybe a fresh hairy coconut, which we broke open with a hammer, drinking its flat tasteless milk and prying out its sweet if tough white heart.

We were always ravenous by suppertime, and no matter what was served we fell on it with relish. Especially on the days when the bread was fresh from the oven. Though Mother would never win any ribbons at the county fair and didn't want to, she did make good bread. And like everybody else (except the elite who could afford the extravagance of bakery bread) she was forced to bake it once a week.

The batter had to be mixed and set to rise the night before. A great, yeasty, bubbling batch in a huge granite pan. Potato water was saved to combine with the scalded milk, salt, sugar, and lard, and into this she sifted white cones of flour. We often knelt on kitchen chairs to watch, begging to help by shaking the heavy, squeaking flour sifter. When the dough was thick and smooth it was covered with a lid and left to rise on the lingering warmth at the back of the stove. If the house was cold, Mother would tuck it down as cozily as she could under a heavy towel.

By morning it would have blossomed tall and white, only to be stirred down and forced to accept more flour. Now she must dump it onto a floured board and knead it, flopping the tough yet delicate mass over and over, pressing out the air bubbles that made little squealing protests, caressing it, yet maneuvering it to her will. And thus subdued it was set to rise again.

By afternoon it was ready to be kneaded once more and molded into loaves. When we were small she always pinched off enough dough to let us play with and to fashion into tiny loaves of our own. They were usually grubby from our hands, but they looked beautiful waiting on the sunny windowsill in the little lids that served as pans. When the loaves themselves had risen, she brushed their plump heads with melted butter and popped them into an oven so hot that sometimes the lids on the range were as rosy as rouged cheeks.

Slowly the heavenly smell of baking bread began to drift through the house. When you came in from school or play your jaws leaked and you began to tease, "When will the bread be done?"

"Well, it should be soon." Opening the nickel-plated door, she would reach in and snap an experimental finger on the brown cracking crust. "Just a few more minutes." Finally, clutching a dish towel, she would reach in and carefully draw out the large black pan. The loaves were dumped on the table, to stand tall and golden as the sheaves of wheat from which the flour had come. Promptly she brushed them with more butter, and they took on a satin sheen. When she broke them apart, their white flesh steamed.

"Now don't eat too much," she would warn as people begged for more. "Hot bread isn't good for the stomach. Besides, I don't want you to spoil your supper."

On rare occasions she diverted part of the batch into cinnamon rolls, a special treat. But the fresh bread itself eaten straight from the oven with butter, or slavered with honey or strawberry jam or apple butter, was enough to rouse the envy of the gods.

In a day or two it was simply bread, no longer so white and a trifle heavy, to be cut on a breadboard with a sawtoothed knife before each meal. And you disloyally wished you could buy bakery bread like some people, it seemed so light and spongy beside your mother's sturdy product.

Mother also made a marvelous bread pudding dignified by the name of "chocolate soufflé." Dry bread soaked in scalded milk; sugar, cocoa, vanilla and a couple of eggs added. Baked in a moderate oven until a knife came clean and its rich chocolaty promise was scarcely to be borne. The crowning touch was the hard sauce, which one of us always made. Confectioners' sugar was stirred into about half a cup of butter, added and pressed and added and pressed until you achieved a fat white ball that could literally take no more. (Also a few drops of vanilla.) Then you made it into individual balls, and stamped on each, with the bottom of a cut-glass toothpick holder, the imprint of a diamond or a daisy or a star. Bread pudding? Nonsense. These creamy balls, melting down over each crusty steaming dish, achieved ambrosia.

But whatever we ate for supper, whether the fare was feast or famine, certain rules prevailed: The whole family ate in the dining room, on a linen cloth with linen napkins. Nobody ever sat down before Mother. And nobody ever left the table unless she excused him first. Nor did we ever begin until everyone was present and until the blessing was asked. Also, we all had to sit straight in our chairs, left hand in the lap. No reaching, no stooping or slurping, and every request prefaced by "please." Mother believed in the old saw: "Always eat as if you were dining with the king, then you'll never be embarrassed if the king comes to dine."

After manners, we shed all pretense of trying to please the king. We were noisy—oral, vocal, clamorous, everybody trying to tell what had happened to *him* today. "Don't talk with your mouth full," Mother kept admonishing. "Don't all try to talk at once." It was futile; good or bad we were dying to spill it at the family table, where we knew reactions would be fervent. The best times were when everybody was in a good mood and the tales were funny. We laughed, sometimes so hard we had to be excused. Dad and my brothers were all incurable clowns; given the slightest encouragement they did what they could to bring this about. Sometimes we burst into song. "Now we don't sing at the table" was another somewhat futile admonition. When people who enjoy each other's company get together it's hard to curb such a spontaneous expression.

Not that harmony always prevailed. The king would have been shocked at the vehemence of our arguments, the sound and fury of our quarrels. When the yelling got too bad Mother would simply say firmly, "I think you'd better be excused." The only things we were not free to discuss at the table were matters which might turn the stomach. No gory details of accidents or operations, no mention of creatures that crawled. If anyone slipped, Dad would pale slightly, clap a napkin to his mouth and flee without even asking Mother.

Other than this, the family's evening meal was a kind of funfest, open forum, wailing wall, and free-for-all. A place where you laughed or complained about your unfair teacher or got very mad and had things out with somebody without missing a bite, or, as far as I know, getting indigestion. A place so lively and filled with possibilities, in fact, that nobody wanted to miss it . . .

Today's experts warn that only agreeable subjects should be discussed at the family dinner table. I suppose I must agree. If and when you can *find* a table with an entire family gathered around it of an evening, the occasion is so rare it ought not to be marred with dissension. I have also read articles describing a kind of protocol of participation. Mother or Father suggests, "Now let's all go around the table and each of us tell the most interesting thing that happened to him or that he's learned today." This too I have tried, with discouraging results. "Aw, nothing much," one child will shrug. Or another, "Sorry, I've got to get going, Mike's picking me up—" While another is intent only poking down the absolute minimum required before escaping back to his programs.

No, the call "Supper's ready!" doesn't echo through neighborhoods much any more. It's dinner now in most places, and it's seldom ready for everybody at the same time. In the first place, Mother's not always there to get it. She's not home from work yet, or the golf course or her club; but there's plenty of food in the refrigerator, or the kids can heat up a nourishing four-course TV dinner, they won't starve. Or Dad's late getting home, and what with bucking traffic after a hard day he needs to unwind a bit. So the clever wife already has the martinis ready, and they share their Happy Hour while the kids eat in the kitchen or the rec room in front of the TV set.

In fact a lot of young wives recommend this as one way to keep a good marriage going. "I always feed the children first;

then Jim and I can enjoy a quiet dinner without all that confusion. We need to be able to talk to each other, we need adult conversation."

Well, fine, good—don't we all? But aren't we already reaping a sorry but logical harvest of kids who were herded off the scene to communicate only with each other, and so can have no meaningful dialogue with adults now? Or who sat transfixed (as children are squatting still) before cartoons and Westerns and wars. No wonder so many of them are violent and destructive, so many of them rude. And how about their manners? How can you learn to sit or stand up straight while slouched on the floor? Who teaches you not to slurp or behave crudely or refrain from discussing the dissection of a worm while eating, if at the same time you're downing a solitary dinner to the accompaniment of pools of blood in living color?

Suppertime . . . That final meal when the day was almost over. The tradition of the family table. In letting it slip away from us I'm afraid we've lost something precious. We've cheated our children, stunted their social growth, gagged their articulation, cut off too early those ties that nature meant for us. The ties that bind us to people in the same family, people who represent comfort, security, nourishment, not only of body but of spirit. Ties that used to be gathered up at the close of day and drawn together, if not always in peace, at least in fellowship and caring. . . .

I wish that by some magic I could step to the door and hear it echoing from every house for blocks. *"Suppertime! Come on in, supper's ready!"*

Going to Church with a Daughter

How nice it is to go to church with a daughter, Lord. What a lovely thing, whether she's two or ten or twenty.

What a blessing, the Sunday morning rites of dressing. Even the inevitable commotion about what to wear. Even the inevitable men's scolding about being late.

Thank you, Lord, for the pleasure of setting off at last and of slipping into a pew feeling—pretty. For a daughter is like wearing a personal adornment, a piece of shining jewelry or a living flower.

People smile upon us. They pay her compliments, which are in essence mine too. For a daughter is a kind of special tribute, an achievement, a joyous adjunct and projection of mother.

Thank you for the privilege of kneeling beside this daughter, reading the responses together, finding the place for her. Or when she's older and I can't find my glasses, having her sure finger find the place for me.

What a blessing, to sing the hymns together. To join voices in the old familiar tunes, or struggle with the new ones. To have eyes meet sometimes, puzzled or in amusement, and remember how my mother and I used to exchange these glances in church together long ago.

Thank you for the special harmony there is between mothers and daughters in church together, Lord, whatever our differences at home. Thank you for this wonderful way to begin the week.

The Son Who Won't Study

Lord, help me to be more understanding of my children's limitations. Guard me against demanding more of them than they are equipped to give.

This son, so bright about anything mechanical, who's up half the night with his ham radio, and is always grubby from rebuilding cars. He's failing in school because he simply won't study. Except for motoring magazines, he won't even *read*.

You know how hard I've tried. Trips to the library, books of his own. I've nagged, scolded, coaxed, pleaded, threatened, offered rewards. And now that they say he's not going to pass, I've stormed.

I shudder at that memory, Lord. My yelling—and his furious, half-bitter, half-bewildered retorts. And that last accusation before he slammed off: "I can't help it, Mom. Stop trying to make me into something I'm not!"

Something he's not . . . and never will be. A professional man like his father. A lover of books and language like me . . . How much he'll *miss*, my very soul grieves. But am I grieving so much for him as for myself?

How can he "miss" something that's alien to his nature, that he's never enjoyed? Any more than I "miss" the things so vital to him? I'm lucky to get a car started, let alone cope with its insides. The very idea of greasy engines is revolting to me . . . What if somebody tried to force me to build a radio?

Help me to see his side of it, Lord, as I sit now in what seems the wreckage of my dreams for my son—and yes, my pride. Help me not to consider what *I* want for him, but what *you* want for him. Since you made him so different from us you must have had your reasons. Help me to understand those reasons and release him to go his different way.

Maybe he's meant to go to trade school instead of high school or college. If so, let me remember how many bright and wonderful people have worked with their hands and haven't gone to college, and how much they've done for the world.

Dear Lord, instead of bemoaning my son's lacks, let me be grateful for his accomplishments. His excellent mind that comprehends things I can't. His skillful hands. Thank you for these gifts, God. Give me new pride in them, and help me to convey that pride to him.

I now accept my son for what he is and can be. I affirm and claim a happy, productive life for him.

A Mother's Wish-Gifts for Christmas

The family has all scattered on errands, Lord, and at last I can wrap their presents. But now, as I sit in this bright clutter of paper and ribbons, I keep thinking of other things, better things, I wish I could give them.

First, I'd love to put peace, world peace in a package. (What a marvelous present for all families everywhere that would be.) But since I can't, maybe I can try even harder to keep peace within this house. To manage less-hectic meals and bedtimes, to prevent or calm down its arguments and conflicts.

Help me in this, Lord.

And this fishing rod I'm struggling to make look nice for my husband, without revealing its secret. What would I like its clumsy package to include?

Freedom to *go* fishing more often, for one thing. But mostly freedom from worry. Worry about mortgages and car payments; about our health, the children's future, our happiness.

But as I sit pondering this impossible gift, you make me realize I *can* give him something very important that will help achieve that very thing: My consideration. Doing everything within my power to spare him.

Our sons, Lord. What would I like to tuck into their boxes along with the boots and shirts and football gear? For one of them, self-confidence, belief in his own abilities, more ease with girls. For the other, better grades so he'll get into the college he wants to attend.

How can I compensate for these gifts that I can't bestow? By more encouragement, more praise, by showing them every day how much I believe in them.

And my daughters, Lord. As I wrap the sweaters and tennis rackets, the books and records, the doll clothes I stayed up so late to finish for the littlest one . . . I can think of so much more I'd hand them if I could.

I'd like to give them poise and graciousness. Kindness and compassion. Courage for all occasions—for tests and dates and interviews, but especially the courage to be themselves whether it makes them popular or not.

Above all, I'd like to say, "Open your eyes and your arms to this priceless present: the wonder of being a woman today when so many careers are calling and you can still be a wife and mother if you want."

The list of my longings for my family is endless, Lord. I can't wrap up the things I really want. But one thing I can give all of them—though no box would ever be big enough to hold it. Something that's mine alone to give, as often as I want:

My love.

Shopping with a Daughter

Lord, please give me strength for this shopping trip with my daughter.

Bless us both and let your love shine through us as we set off on what should be so pleasant, but is generally such an ordeal.

First, fortify me with thanksgiving. I realize I am lucky to have a lovely, healthy daughter who really enjoys clothes. And lucky to have enough money (if we don't go overboard) to provide the things she needs.

But I'm going to need some extra fortifying, Lord, with the following:

Please give me patience as we trudge from store to store, parade in and out of fitting rooms. (Ease my aching feet, soothe my frazzled nerves, keep sweet before me the picture of that hour when she finally finds *something* that meets with her approval.)

Give me will power. Don't let me show enthusiasm (if I like anything she's sure to shudder). Help me refrain from even making suggestions. No, however difficult, help me stand quietly by and let her choose.

Above all, don't let me talk her into things. And if I have to talk her *out* of things, please give me tact, let me be kind but firm. And let her accept my reasons without being too disappointed or resentful.

Give me good sense about price tags, God. Don't let me

spoil her. But don't let me spoil our relationship either by being a pinchpenny mother.

Remind us both to smile at each other. To discuss instead of argue. To laugh when we're practically on the verge of blows. And to take time out for lunch or a cup of coffee. (It's when we both get tired that nerves and tempers flare.)

Thank you for giving us both strength for this shopping trip. For the joy and anticipation I suddenly feel. I'm smiling at her already, and she's smiling back! We do love each other enough to overcome our problems and appreciate our good fortune. We're setting off today to discover new delights.

Thank you that I can go shopping with my daughter!

A Boy's First Car

Dear Lord, please bless this boy and his first car.

Bless his pride in it, his joy in it, his plans for it.

Let it be whole and sound and right and good for him. Let it carry him safely.

Lord, bless his energies—may they be equal to cope with it (and pay for it).

Bless his mind—may it learn from the mechanical experiences he will have with this car. And may he learn from the emotional experiences this car is going to bring.

Oh, God, give my son judgment in operating this car.

Give him joy without recklessness, power without folly.

Give him generosity and dignity and decency and common sense.

Lord, I offer them up to you for blessing and safe-keeping: This boy. This car.

I Can't Understand My Daughter
Any More

I just can't understand my daughter any more, God. And she can't understand me.

We used to be so close, we used to be such friends. Even when we had our differences she'd come flying back to me.

But now, though there are still moments of sweetness and laughter, times when we can talk, those times are so few. I don't understand her silences, Lord, her locked door, the secrets she keeps from me. And when we do talk there is so much crossness and tension and criticism. Often outright hostility.

Where has my little girl gone, God? What have I done to drive her away?

And you, Lord, seem to tell me:

She's going where you went, where all girls go: To find herself. And you haven't driven her away. Life is beckoning to her, and she must follow. This is what you've really been preparing her for, isn't it? To be strong enough to find her way.

But it hurts, God. I love her so much. Why must she make it so hard for me?

And clear and true I hear the answer. The only possible answer: *Because it is so wonderful having a daughter. Otherwise, you couldn't bear to let her go!*

The Lovely Aliens

Oh, Lord, please bless these lovely aliens, my children.

They seem so strange to me at times, not even resembling me in face or traits or body.

It is sometimes hard to believe that I had anything to do with producing them, these vigorous strangers going their own way with such vigor and independence.

The fact that I even clothe and care for them seems an anomaly, as if I am just some loving outsider attending their needs.

At times I protest this, Lord. I don't want to be an outsider.

I am lonely for the deeper attachments we had when they were small. I feel a hungry desire to know more truly what they think, to share their lives.

A kind of righteous indignation rises up, demanding, "See here, if it weren't for me you wouldn't *be* here! Pay attention to me, draw me in. Darnit, I'm your *mother*."

Then I am reminded of my own, often inconsiderate youth.

You help me to see that this is nature's way, however cruel, of cutting natal strings. I cannot carry them forever in my womb, or on my lap. (Only in my heart.)

The burden of it would be intolerable. For my sake as well as theirs, I've got to let them alone, let them go.

So bless them as they make these fierce, sometimes foolish, sometimes faltering strides toward independence. Give them strength—they're going to need it!

Don't let my self-pity sap their progress. God bless these lovely aliens, my children.

Rescue This Child

Oh, God, please help my child. He has no direction, no goal. He's wandered away from so much that he used to be, or that you, his creator, would have him be.

And I am not only worried sick about this, God, I feel guilty. I search my own behavior asking, "Why? Why? What have I done to bring this about? Where have we, his family, failed?" That he, with all his goodness and beauty, his brains, his tremendous potential, should be so lost. Right now it's as if he's nobody going nowhere, at a time when the rest of the world is on its way.

Dear God, please find and restore my wandering child. Arouse in him a sense of purpose, steady him, set him upon his rightful path, and walk with him.

We who love him can't do it. Only you who love him even more can do it.

I offer him to you now, whole and beautiful and filled with promise, the way you sent him to us. Thank you for helping him become the person you meant him to be.

Respite

Oh, Lord, thank you for this little space between crises in our family. Thank you for this probably brief span of peace.

Right now nobody is ill. Thank you. Right now nobody is in trouble. Thank you. Right now I am coasting, resting. It is as if I am walking across a pleasant meadow with only the happy chiming of birds in my ears and the sunlight as of some wondrous love upon my face.

The familiar cries of sorrow, distress, imploring pleas, and arguments are still. Thank you. The familiar burdens seem to be lifted, the problems for the moment all resolved. I rejoice in this sense of lightness and release.

It is common sense that tells me that this lovely respite cannot last, and not really my lack of faith.

For now, let me simply be thankful for this respite. Let me be revitalized by it. Let me draw from it physical strength and spiritual resources for the inevitable crises and conflicts to come.

Thank you, God, for this precious span of peace.

Psalm for a Sister

I will lift up my eyes and smile as I give thanks for my sister. My radiant, complicated sister, who is more than a sister—who is my friend. (Blessed is the woman who has one like her, and thrice blessed if she has more than one.)

I will thank the good Lord that we were children together, sharing the same room and for years the same bed.

I am grateful for the memory of her small body warm against mine. I rejoice to remember our playhouses and paper dolls and plans. Our secrets and surprises. Even our quarrels.

I feel a deep and poignant longing for those days when we were girls together. Life-hungry, love-hungry, each fighting her own battle, yet supporting each other against parents and the world.

My sister, oh Lord, my beautiful sister, often maddening, always understanding, always fun.

Thank you for this woman who shares my parents, my past, my blood; who sees me whole—the beginning, long ago, and the person I am now. My sister, whose faults are so clear to me—and dear to me, just as my faults are to her. Yet for all our differences, and the miles that lie between us, we would still battle the world for each other.

I laugh for the joy of my sister, all the comedy, the gaiety. And I sometimes weep for my sister. I long to comfort her, to hold her close, as we held each other for comfort or for courage as little girls.

Dear God, please take good care of her, this sister I love so much.

The Earth's Heart Beating

How can I find you, God? How can I claim your strength?

I am tired, so tired . . . tense, so tense. And my nerves are screaming. Now, if ever, I need you. I need your reassurance and your peace.

Yet there is only this raw trembling vacancy inside me. This sense of emptiness and futility.

Come back to me, Lord. Calm me, quiet me, for I am indeed weary and heavy-laden and I need your promised rest.

"Stop going so hard, Mother," a daughter says. "Lie down a few minutes, relax."

I flop on the floor and she kneels beside me, long and lithe and fair, and deftly massages my neck and back. "Let yourself go. Be like the cat."

It dozes on the arm of a chair, eyes half closed. I stretch out . . . and out . . . trying to emulate its yawning movements. . . . How utterly cats yield every muscle and nerve, how sweetly they sleep. But how do they occupy themselves all day? I wonder. Nobody to play with, nobody to talk to, nothing to think about. Yet this cat of ours goes outside and vanishes for hours . . . must surely occupy itself with something for hours. Chases a bird or a rabbit, suns itself, prowls the woods . . . How stupendously boring—unless you are a cat.

I ponder some of this aloud, and my daughter, who has left my side, looks up from the jeans she is mending.

"She's in tune with the universe," she says. "God keeps her happy."

"Why? I wonder. Why a cat at all?"

"God put her here to be company to us, and perhaps to teach us that. That the way to be happy is just not to worry, to relax, to flow with the universe."

"But people can't do that. We have too many problems, things to worry about."

"Yes, but the animals have their problems, too," she says. "Most of them. The mere problem of survival. And they're calm about the whole thing, they trust nature—their own nature and the larger nature all around them."

"People are different. We can't be like that."

"Yes, we can. Some people do. People who take up the religious life and just meditate, or take vows of silence. It's the same thing, just merging with the universe."

"That seems selfish. It's escaping responsibilities to other people."

"I think nature meant us to be more selfish than most people are. What's really more important than the self, Mother? You yourself? The problems go away, most of them, but you remain. You stay *you*. You shouldn't let yourself get so damaged and divided up by responsibilities and problems."

Thoughtfully she bites a thread. "I pray about things, so many things, so many problems. I know I don't have half so many responsibilities as you—yet I think I have a lot, for my time of life I do. And I pray about the people and the problems, and then I try to meditate, but that takes mental effort. It's better when I just let go, just relax and let myself flow into nature—the rain, for instance. The rain speaks to me almost as if it's trying to tell me something. Last night it was raining and I prayed and pretty soon it was the rain praying with me, and almost the rain praying *for* me. I could just lie there and listen.

"And there are times when I have just lain out in the sun and on the grass and flowed into it, the universe—and I could hear the earth's heart beating."

"The earth's heart?"

"Yes, don't you think God put some of his own heart into the earth when he made it? And gave it a heart, too?"

(Out of the mouths of babes, I think . . . or a daughter twenty-two . . . No, wisdom is not reserved solely for the old.)

The earth's heart beating . . . and my own. Yes.

For now as I lie here resting, yielded as the cat, it comes to me through my own hand, that steady pulsing . . . and hers . . . and that of the quiet cat.

For are we not all one? Linked to the same rhythms, we three creatures within this room . . . and all those beyond. Seen and unseen, the blood flows, life-sustaining.

Within the very earth itself the currents flow. The vital life forces of all its inhabitants and the saps and juices of all its vegetation reaching down and up. And in and through and deeper, ever deeper, the ceaseless silent pounding of energies undreamed.

A sense of joyous discovery fills me.

For I realize now that to sense it and become one with its source I must stop struggling. To fight with life is to fight off God!

Now I feel his presence, his reality, his strength.

Now I hear the quiet rhythms and am cradled in those rhythms like a child being rocked to sleep. . . . Now I can truly rest.

We Are Moving Again, and
I Don't Want to Go

We are moving again, God, and I don't want to go.

I am sick and tired of moving.

I resent the time that must be squandered in packing and unpacking. In house selling and house hunting.

I don't want the children to have to change schools anymore. I don't want to have to make new friends anymore. I don't want to have to explain myself anymore, or try to find myself (or even my way around) in a new setting.

The adventure of moving has palled, Lord.

Setting off for a new city I used to think, "Somewhere out there it lies waiting for us. There in its vastness stands the place that will become home to us. There, right now, laughing and talking, are the people who will become important to us."

But now, oh Lord, this same prospect fills me only with a sense of being lost. Wanderers, strangers, with no real home to go to. Not really belonging anywhere, to anyone.

I have a sudden shocked awareness of how Mary and Joseph must have felt that night when they faced the careless crowds of Bethlehem and were told to be on their way.

I want to be able to put my roots down. Deep, deep.

How can I ever find out who I am if, so much of my life, I don't even know *where* I am?

Oh, God, hang onto me once more as I face the chaos and confusion of moving.

Help me to realize that you will go with us again, you will be with us again. I can talk to you wherever I am; I have a friend I can never lose in you wherever I am.

God, sustain me as I face this move.

The Farewell Party

Thank you, God, for all these people who have gathered to tell us good-bye.

The ones we've been so close to and the ones we've rarely seen. The ones we've liked so much and even the ones who've been sometimes hard to take.

Now curiously, they are all dear to us as we come together for the farewell party. Now suddenly I see who they are in relation to us—and who we must be in relation to them.

They are the living embodiment of time and place—our time in this particular place. They are themselves, yes, but in large or small ways they are changed because we came together. And we are changed because of them. We have interrelated; the precious stuff of our lives has touched.

What a miracle this is, what a blessing. That you created us, not to live alone or behind closed doors, but to brush against and help to color other lives.

And when this time is over, the parting hurts.

Friends taken for granted become strangely precious when it is time to separate.

Perhaps this is why these partings must come. To make us aware of each other, to realize our identities as characters in each other's life stories. To give us a little glimpse of who we are in the eyes of those who are our friends.

A farewell party—what a joy, however it hurts. What an

honor. They love us enough to wish us well. "Fare well wherever you go," they are saying.

And we can only answer in kind, "Good-bye. Fare . . . well."

Thank you for all these dear people, Lord. And bring us together again in another place, another time.

"Give Me a Bright Word, Mother"

Our daughter has always loved words.

From the time she was beginning to talk she was forever chanting them, trying out strange combinations, as if fascinated by their very sound. And when she had started to school and was learning to read and write words of her own, words assumed some lovely new significance.

She was impatient because her vocabulary was still too small to express all the things she was discovering, and so she began asking for words as she might ask for cookies or a hug. Words became a form of favor, a kind of little gift that only I, who used them in my work, could bestow.

Waking up in the morning, or rushing in from play, she would ask: "Give me a bright word, Mother."

And I would answer with a little string of words—object or adjective—that called up brightness to the senses or the mind: "Sunshine . . . Golden . . . Luminous . . . Shiny, like a fire engine that's just been polished. Or jewelry . . . Sparkling . . . Diamonds sparkling in a golden crown."

"Is luminous bright and shiny like a pan? Is that why they call some pans *aluminum?*"

"It could be, but I don't think so. Aluminum is a little too shiny for luminous. I think of luminous as more like moonlight shining on a lake or through the leaves."

"Oh, I love luminous!" she would cry. Decisively, like a shopper: "I'll take luminous."

Or the request would be: "Give me a soft word, Mother."

"Velvety," I'd begin. "Velvety soft like a blackberry or a pony's nose. Or furry, like your kitten . . . Or how about lull-aby? That's a nice soft word . . . Or soothing . . . Gentle . . . Dreamy."

Her own eyes would go soft and dreamy with listening. She would try them on her tongue, murmuring, "Gentle . . . vel-vety . . . soooothing." With a little sigh—"That's nice—soooothing. That's my word!"

Or, perhaps cross or frustrated, she would come storming in from play. "I need a glad word right now!"

"Glad? All right, let's see. Circus is a glad word. Circus clowns, parades . . . Or how about birthday? Presents. Sur-prises. Party . . . And some glad words to go with them are joy, excitement, laughter, fun."

"No, no, I already *have* those words," she would sometimes protest.

"Well then, jubilee. That means a glorious celebration. And another glad word that sounds a lot like it is jubilant . . . Or maybe you'd like elated?"

Taking them in, savoring them, her face would brighten. "Oh," she would marvel, "it must be wonderful to know so many words!"

She outgrew all this, of course. Before long words had ceased to awe her. She has acquired plenty of words of her own, a whole vast treasury of words to use as she needs or pleases. Words for diaries and letters and to spill to friends on the phone. Words for school reports and tests. Words in books that she has to read or wants to. And if the meaning of any of these words eludes her she has a dictionary handy, she can al-ways look them up.

No, my daughter no longer must come rushing to me like an eager little shopper seeking words to fit her moods.

And yet, in another far more vital and challenging sense she still turns to me, expectant, convinced I'll be able to provide the words she needs:

"I want to be in with these kids, I want to be popular, but I still want to be myself. How can I do both, Mother? . . ."

"Is there any way I can make this teacher *believe* I didn't cheat? . . ."

"How can I tell Daddy what I did to the car? . . ."

"Why won't you let me go? Everybody else is allowed. . . ."

"I don't care what she's done or what they say, she's my friend and we've got to help her, Mother. . . ."

"Why doesn't he call? Oh, Mommy, what'll I *do* if he doesn't like me any more? . . ."

The times when she's puzzled or tempted or troubled, the times when her heart is breaking. The times when she can't understand. Then, in spite of all the words I've read and said and heard and think I know, I find myself groping desperately for the right ones. I feel like the child she used to be, running up to me with her demands.

I too need a source that is older and wiser. And I find myself imploring: "Give me a hope word. Give me a sure word. Give me a bright word, God!"

He Was So Young

He was so young, God.

So young and strong and filled with promise. So vital, so radiant, giving so much joy wherever he went.

He was so brilliant. On this one boy you lavished so many talents that could have enriched your world. He had already received so many honors, and there were so many honors to come.

Why, then? In our agony we ask. Why him?

Why not someone less gifted? Someone less good? Some hop-head, rioter, thief, brute, hood?

Yet we know, even as we demand what seems to us a rational answer, that we are only intensifying our grief. Plunging deeper into the blind and witless place where all hope is gone. A dark lost place where our own gifts will be blunted and ruin replace the goodness he brought and wished for us.

Instead, let us thank you for the marvel that this boy was. That we can say good-bye to him without shame or regret, rejoicing in the blessed years he was given to us. Knowing that his bright young life, his many gifts, have not truly been stilled or wasted, only lifted to a higher level where the rest of us can't follow yet.

Separation? Yes. Loss? Never.

For his spirit will be with us always. And when we meet him again we will be even more proud.

Thank you for this answer, God.

For a Daughter About to Be Married

Listen, Lord, please listen . . .

I am very conscious of you as I stand beside my daughter's bed. She is tired from all the preparations; she has turned in early. But I can't sleep. I have slipped in to tuck up the covers about her one more time. And to just stand here a moment absorbing her loveliness.

Tomorrow she is to be married—this baby that came to us at such an inconvenient time.

I know you have long since forgiven me for how dismayed and resentful I was then. I know you have been with us since, sharing our almost passionate pride and pleasure in her accomplishments. (You heard my thanks, you know my sense of blessing.)

You have been close to us too in the times of anguish, the illnesses, the arguments, the problems. (You heard and answered my prayers.)

Now I want to thank you once again for all those years that she has been a part of our family and has meant so much to us.

Bless her tomorrow as she stands beside the young man who is her final choice. Be with her as she makes her solemn promises. Stay close to her as she begins this new life that is her own, separate and apart from us.

Give her joy and pride in her husband; and him in her.

Lord, I could ask so many things for both of them. I could ask that you spare them trials, hardships, differences, sorrows. And I do ask that—yes, I suppose, even knowing that they will have their share.

Now I ask only that the companionship surpass the conflicts, the happiness far outweigh the hurts. And that whatever they face, they both stay close to you.

And oh, yes, one final thing, Lord, as I tuck her in this last time and turn away: May every child she bears bring her the delight that she has brought to us.

Don't Let Me Cry
at the Wedding

Oh, Lord, don't let me cry at my little girl's wedding.

Don't let me cry as she comes down the aisle.

Let the radiance she has given our lives shine on my face now, to match the radiance on hers.

Let her feel, not my aching sense of loss, but my joy that she has found so fine a man to take care of her for us.

Oh, Lord, don't let my husband hurt at our daughter's wedding.

That arm that she's clinging to as proudly, trustingly, as when she was a little girl—thank you for it.

Let this be truly a moment of communion for them, a happy summary of all their memories as father and daughter.

Thank you for the steadiness of his step and the pride in his eyes as he gives her away.

Thank you for his smile as he takes his place beside me. For permitting us to come to this hour together, surrounded by so many people dear to us, to witness this beautiful ceremony.

My heart is full of thanksgiving. Almost too full of wonder and blessing. I love her so and rejoice so for her.

Lord, don't let me cry at my little girl's wedding.

Give Me the Love
to Let Them Go

Lord, sometimes I love my children so much it seems I can't ever bear to let them go.

"Hurry back!" my heart cries after them almost every time they leave, whether for camp or a date or just the daily trudging off down the walk for school.

No matter what the confusion we've just been through—the frantic scramble for books or money or a missing sweater, no matter the chaos, the noise, even the quarrels, something inside me goes scurrying after them with last minute words of love and warning. And the urgent unspoken plea: "Come back soon."

And when they are all gone at once, God, like right now . . . Though you know how I revel in the peace and freedom, yet there is this aching emptiness inside me too.

And sometimes, alone with their father, I have this sense of some awful preview: Of loneliness and boredom. Of a life without purpose and meaning. Of two people haunting the mailbox for letters, or waiting for the phone to ring . . . Or worse, a couple clinging to an unmarried son or daughter, unwilling to let the last one leave.

Lord, thank you for making me aware of this dread presentiment. It's like a signal telling me I've got to start weaning myself from my children. Not loving them any less, but ceasing to feast so continually on all they do. I realize I've got to start nourishing myself in other ways. New interests apart from them—help me to find them, God, starting now. Spur me to call that class I've been thinking of joining, that volunteer service that needs me. Things that will help me to grow as a person. There are a hundred unlocked doors and opportunities in my life, things I want to explore, things that challenge.

Now is the time to anticipate them. Now is the time to start finding them. Don't let me make excuses for myself—how busy I am, how much the children still need me. And guard me from these guilty, doubtful feelings already beginning to stir.

Brace me with the knowledge that the kindest, most generous thing I can do for my family is to begin to prepare for the time when they won't be coming back. A time when they won't have to feel guilty or selfish about poor old Mom whose world has collapsed.

Thank you for this insight, God. Give me the love to let my children go.

Bring Back the Children

Lord, it seems sometimes that my arms aren't long enough or my lap isn't big enough. I wish I could stretch my arms out and out to embrace all my children. These, here about the table now, and those who are away, off to their meetings or their dates or far away in their own homes.

I am suddenly aware of them, all of them wherever they are, and the excitement and wonder and pain of their lives are almost too much to comprehend.

I am so thrilled about them, so proud of them, and so worried about them too—all at once. I want suddenly to reach out and touch them, the warmth of their flesh, the feel of their hair, to draw them physically in.

I want to hold them on my lap again, the big ones and the little ones, all at once. I want to tuck them in their beds under the same familiar roof. I want to lock the door and go to sleep knowing they're all safe in the shelter of this house.

Lord, I wish I could have all my children back—now, this moment, at once. But since I can't, you who are everywhere, reach them for me, keep them safe in the shelter of my love.

First Grandchild

Thank you, God, that it's here, it's here, our first grandchild!

I hang up the telephone, rejoicing. I gaze out the window, dazzled and awed. "Just a few moments ago," he said. "A beautiful little girl."

She arrived with the sunrise, Lord. The heavens are pink with your glory. Radiance streams across the world.

The very trees lift up their branches as if in welcome, as if to receive her. And I want to fling out my arms, too, in joy and gratefulness and welcome.

My arms and my heart hold her up to you for blessing.

Oh, Lord, thank you for her and bless her, this little new life that is beginning its first day.

The Letter Home

All over the world tonight women sit writing: The brides, still a trifle self-conscious as they perform this new domestic task; the wives so long married it has become second nature—writing the letter home.

"Dear Mother and Dad— Well, we made it. It was a long hard trip, but so wonderful I want to tell you all about it. Jim was so sweet. No girl ever had a lovelier honeymoon."

Or, "Dear folks: I'll try to snatch a little time while the baby's napping, to report on what's been happening." Or, "Dear Families—including Margaret and Elmer, Grandpa and Grandma, Bob and Uncle Mac: Please forgive me for the carbon copies. Have been so frantically busy that the only way to catch up on our correspondence is to write to everybody at once."

And typed or handwritten, on finest stationery or the back of a child's wobbly drawing, they have a quality all their own —a woman's letters home.

For she has left her own people to follow her man. And whether they have moved just a few hundred miles away or across a continent, an ocean, her letters trace the course of her new life. A life filled with all the incidents, great and small, that go into the fabric of a family: The first tooth and the first operation. The raise in salary, the Couples' Club they've joined, the church, the grocery store, the neighbors. The hopes, the prospects, the aspirations; and often—though these are touched on lightly, if mentioned at all—the disappointments and worries.

For slowly, subtly, a woman senses that this is a record of happiness, actually, her letter home. Not that she is expected to write only of sunshine and roses. Nor that she's too proud to complain. No, it's something deeper, more significant. A gradual recognition that, however she may put it off, a wonderful thing happens when she sits down to write that letter home.

For this is her journal, her account. And strangely, it is the good, the gay, the funny things that come swimming to the surface of the chaos of raising a family. By a kind of magic, in the sheer act of recollecting and recounting, her own appreciation takes over, her confidence in the future, her gratefulness. Seldom does she consciously think: "I won't write that. It would worry them." Rather, the problem doesn't seem so bad in retrospect—and less interesting than Sue's first formal and Ted's paper route.

Her words are awaited hopefully all over the world, on farms, in cities, in little towns. No author, however famous, has an audience more eager, more faithful. Day after day, parents watch for the letters, fret when they don't arrive, wondering what's wrong. And oh, the rejoicing, the lift of the spirits when they do. "Here it is. Well, it's about time! Let's see what Alice has to say."

So women sit writing. Up and down the street, in the big cities and the small towns, all over the world. Writing that diary of their destiny, making their entry into the account books of their lives: "Dear Folks . . ." "Dear Mother and Dad . . ."

Mothers Keep All These Things

But Mary kept all these things, and pondered them in her heart.

ST. LUKE

You make your annual pilgrimage to the attic to bring down the decorations from the family Christmas box. The long ropes of tinsel for the tree. The fragile colored balls, a few always shattered. The faded big red stocking that's hung on the front door how many years? The crèche and its figures—Baby Jesus in the tiny cradle that the youngest ones love, the wise men, the shepherds—they are getting grubby, you notice, and one of the kneeling camels has lost an ear.

Really, you should replace so many things. Take this stable, just a rough box on which one of the boys nailed a clumsy roof. Or that angel—too big for the scene; an awkward plaster angel your little girl made and painted with watercolors in second grade. Surely you should throw it out—she'd never miss it. You reach for the wastebasket, drop it in. But suddenly, with the compulsion that makes you rush back to the fireplace to rescue their papers or drawings, you haul it forth again. You can't do it. Because, though its creator would never miss her lumpy angel—you would.

Mary kept all these things, and pondered them in her heart—

How many things a mother keeps, you think as you look about . . . Battered little first books. Baby shoes. Scrapbooks stuffed with their pictures and souvenirs. A daughter's first

]117[

prom dress . . . Such foolish things that only a mother would cling to. All mothers. Mothers like Mary, who have gone before—and mothers to come.

"Keepsakes," is written on a large box on the shelf. And in it, lovingly labeled by fingers long still, is a yellow sailor suit that belonged to the child who grew up to be your husband. His own first laboriously printed Christmas cards. And his first pair of red boots. His mother, too, kept all these things. When we were first married I used to wonder why. Then I had a child, and I understood.

Mothers keep all these things. Because they are the physical reminders of our children, the shed garments of a time that, however hectic it may be now, will someday seem precious.

Mary kept all these things . . .

You feel a renewed kinship for that girl-mother. You wonder what reminders of His childhood did she perhaps save. His first little garments, or the sandals in which He learned to walk? A wooden toy cart perhaps, that His father had made for him in the carpenter shop? And what memories did they bring back to her later to ponder in her heart?

You take up the bulging box. This year, as usual, its contents will all make the journey into the holiday with the family. The lumpy angel, the battered bells, the beloved red stocking, mended and refurbished with a bright new bow. It wouldn't be Christmas otherwise.

Because Christmas is for keeps. It comes every year and will go on forever. And along with Christmas belong the keepsakes and the customs. Those humble, everyday things that a mother clings to with her hands, and ponders, like Mary, in the secret spaces of her heart.

At Christmas,
the Heart Goes Home*

At Christmas, all roads lead home. The filled planes, packed trains, overflowing buses—all speak eloquently of a single destination: home. Despite the crowding, the delays and the confusion, we clutch our bright packages and beam our anticipation. We are like birds driven by an instinct we only faintly understand—the hunger to be with our own.

If we are already snug by our own fireside surrounded by growing children, or awaiting the return of older ones who are away, then the heart takes a side trip. In memory, we journey back to the Christmases of long ago. Once again, we are curled into quivering balls of excitement listening to the mysterious rustle of tissue paper and the tinkle of untold treasures as parents perform their magic on Christmas Eve. Or we recall the special Christmases that are like little landmarks in the life of a family.

One memory is particularly dear to me—a Christmas during the Great Depression when Dad was out of work and the rest of us were scattered. My sister, Gwen, and her husband, Leon, were in another state, expecting their first baby. My brother Harold, an aspiring actor, was traveling with a road show. I was a senior working my way through a small college 500 miles away.

Just before the holidays, my boss had offered me $50—a fortune!—to keep the office open the two weeks he would be

* First appeared in *Guideposts* magazine, December 1976. Reprinted by permission of Guideposts Associates, Inc.

gone. "And boy, do I need the money, Mom. I know you'll understand," I wrote.

I wasn't prepared for her reply: the other kids couldn't make it either! Except for my kid brother, Barney, she and Dad would be alone.

Our first Christmas apart! And as the carols drifted up the dormitory stairs, as the corridors rang with the laughter and chatter of other girls packing to leave, my misery deepened.

Then one night, when the dorm was almost empty, I had a long-distance call. "Gwen!" I gasped. "What's wrong?" (In those days, long distance usually meant an emergency.)

"Listen. Leon's got a new generator and we think the old jalopy can make it home. I've wired Harold. If he can meet us halfway, he can ride with us. But don't tell the folks; we want to surprise them. Marj, you've got to come, too."

"Oh, Gwen, I wish I could. But I just can't leave now."

We hung up, and I went moodily back to my room. Moments later, I was called to the phone again. It was my boss, saying he'd decided to close the office after all. My heart leaped, for it wasn't too late to catch a ride with the girl down the hall. I ran to pound on her door.

They already had a load, she said. But if I was willing to sit on somebody's lap . . . Her dad was downstairs waiting.

It was snowing as we piled into that heaterless car. We drove all night, singing and hugging each other to keep warm. Not minding—how could we? We were going home!

"Marj!" Mother stood in the doorway clutching her robe about her, silver-black hair spilling down her back, eyes large with alarm, then incredulous joy. "Oh, *Marj!*"

I'll never forget those eyes or the feel of her arms around me, so soft and warm after the bitter cold. My feet felt frozen after that drive, but they warmed up as my parents fed me and put me to bed. And when I awoke, it was to the jangle of sleigh bells Dad hung each year on the front door. And voices. My kid brother shouting, "Harold! Gwen! Leon!" The clamor of astonished greetings, the laughter, the kissing, the questions. And then we all gathered around the kitchen table the way we used to, recounting our adventures.

"I had to hitchhike, clear to Peoria," my older brother scolded merrily. "*Me,* the leading man." He lifted an elegant two-toned shoe—with a flapping sole. "In these!"

"But, by golly, you *got* here." Dad's face was beaming. Then suddenly he broke down—Dad who never cried. "We're together!"

For most Christmases since that memorable one, we've been lucky. During the years our children were growing up, there were no separations. Then one year, history repeated itself. For various reasons, not a single, faraway child could get home. Worse, my husband had flown to Florida for some vital surgery. He was adamant about our not coming with him "just because it's Christmas," when he'd be back in another week.

Like my mother before me; I still had one chick left— Melanie, 14. "We'll get along fine," she said, trying to cheer me.

We built a big fire every evening, went to church, wrapped presents, pretended. But the ache in our hearts kept swelling. And the day before Christmas, we burst into mutual tears. "Mommy, it's just not *right* for Daddy to be down there by himself!"

"I know it." I ran to the telephone. The airlines were hopeless, but there was one roomette available on the last train to Miami. Almost hysterical with relief, we threw things into bags.

And what a Christmas Eve! Excited as conspirators we cuddled together in that cozy space. Melanie hung a tiny wreath in the window and we settled down to watch the endless pageantry flashing by the rhythmic clicking song of the rails. Villages and city streets—all dancing with lights and decorations and sparkling Christmas trees. And cars and countrysides and people—all the people. Each one on a special pilgrimage of love and celebration.

At last we drifted off to sleep. But hours later I awoke to a strange stillness. The train had stopped. Raising the shade, I peered out on a small town. Silent, deserted, with only a few lights still burning. And under the bare branches, along a lonely street, a figure was walking. A young man in sailor blues, head bent, hunched under the weight of the seabag on his shoulders. And I thought—*home, he's almost home!* I wondered if there was someone still waiting for him, or if anyone knew he was coming at all. And my heart cried out to him, for he was suddenly my own son and my own ghost, and the soul of us all—driven, so immutably driven, by this annual call, "Come home!"

There must be some deep psychological reason why we turn so instinctively toward home at this special time. Perhaps we are acting out the ancient story of a man and a woman and a coming child, plodding along with their donkey toward their destination. It was necessary for Joseph to return to the city of his birth. The long, arduous trip across the mountains of Judea was also the journey of a life toward birth.

Perhaps it's no wonder, then, that Christmas draws us home. In a way, are we not celebrating *our* birth too? Our journey into life, our meeting with our parents. The first Christmases we knew with people who loved us.

The child who was born on that first Christmas grew to be a man who taught us many important things. But the message that has left the most lasting impression and given the most hope and comfort is this: that we do have a home to go to, that there will be an ultimate homecoming, a place where we will be reunited, forever, with those we love.

Good-by, Christmas Tree

Taking down the Christmas tree is like stripping the feathers from some beautiful bird. Even the children, so eager to do the adorning, escape this chore if they can. And after a dutiful insistence on a mother's part: "You can at least take the ornaments off the lower branches," and (visualizing havoc): "No, dear, I'd rather you didn't climb the stepladder to get the angel off the top," you shoo the children off, privately relieved. Like many another rite of womanhood, this one seems to be a solitary task.

You go about it with vigor, wrapping the bright baubles and stowing them in their boxes; efficiently winding the prickly strands of tinsel; and, with the probable foolish thriftiness that men seldom understand, plucking the frail silver icicles to save them too—as many as you can. How they dance in the still staunchly shining lights! How they cling to the brittle branches and your hand. Small though their actual value, you feel their growing weight like a tangible treasure that is too precious to throw out.

Too precious. The branches reach out their arms. Even the dry tick of their falling needles does not mitigate the sense of some gentle imploring: "Stay, stay!" And though you yourself have said, in the hectic rush of holiday preparations, "Christmas comes too often. I wish we could just skip it every other year," and, in the chaos of papers and presents, "I'll be glad when we can get out of this mess," now you stand haunted by it. The whole of it, from the very beginning. From your first shocked protest, seeing the decorations and hearing the carols

]123[

in the stores: "No, no. It can't be Christmas. Not again! Why do they have to start it so early?" to this moment.

For there was scarcely time for Christmas, after all. The shopping, the cards, the baking, the parties, the programs at church and at school. Almost before you knew it, it was Christmas Eve—and you stand remembering the children's anticipation, so intense it was akin to anguish. And the rattle of wrappings, the squawk of a doll, as you and your husband stuffed stockings, laid out gifts, in the ancient, thrilling parental conspiracy. And the focal point of it all—this lovely tree. Like a queen, the tree graced the window, pouring its rainbow lights upon the snow and welcoming you when you returned from midnight services. And then it was morning, and the youngsters were shouting, "Wake up, wake up! Merry Christmas. Come see!"

How festive it all was, the tree reminds you—the dear, still shining tree. How joyous. Belatedly, you stand there, wanting to stop its plunge into the past. Not let Christmas truly be over—as it will be over and done with, once the tree is down. And with the going of that tree, another year in the life of your family.

Never again will things be just as they are now, with the children just this age. A toddler, a second-grader, a Cub Scout, and a son who has known the thrill of shopping with money from his first paper route. Next year Jimmy will have abandoned his bike for a car, and the daughter who wanted one final doll will be asking for clothes, instead, and be interested in boys.

There will be other gifts, you know, the pleasures and the problems of other stages. But with each passing holiday the children are growing away from you—and, like this tree, will eventually be gone. And you can't wrap their bright, insistent lives in tissue paper and store them in a closet. All you can wrap, to treasure and hold fast, are your memories.

But now, this very Christmas—which you approached with such resistance and found at times so trying. How could I? a mother wonders, standing there alone, gazing at the lights.

They are almost more lovely shining on the bare uncluttered branches. Their strings are like living eyes, blinking merrily. Flooding the tree now in scarlet, now turquoise, gold, and a merry fountain of winking hues.

It is time to hush their bright clamor, time to silence and darken their gay reign. Come now, unplug them. Just a touch of the hand. And as you reluctantly reach out, you bid the tree good-by: "It's been wonderful, hasn't it? Why, it's the very best Christmas we've ever had!"

Mother, I'm Home!

"Mother, where are you? I'm home!" Day after day you hear that call. Over and over. When the littlest bounces in from kindergarten, proudly bearing his crayon drawing: "Mommy, here I am. Look what I made today. Mommy, I'm home!" At three o'clock when the older ones begin to streak in: "Hey, I'm home." Sometimes on weekends or holidays, the ones away at college. "I'm here! It's me. I'm home."

And with that cry come both responsibility and rejoicing. As life begins to surge through the house you take up the tasks it brings. The sandwiches they demand before tearing off for football practice, the money for Cub Scout dues, the things to be found: "Honey, those shoes are right under the bed where you left them." The phone calls: "Mary wonders if Jeanie can stay awhile."

And the day's adventures to be listened to, its triumphs and its disasters: "I made it, I made it. I'm a cheerleader!" "Mom, Miss Johnson promised I could wash the board, but she chose Marie." "Mother, I've just got to talk to you about this boy."

It's a signal that peace is ended, that cry "I'm home." With the banging of the door, your day is stirred once again to action. No longer are you your own person. You belong to them.

Yet, in the confidence of that cry, you feel a surge of pride. They want you; they seek you out. However poorly equipped you may feel for the job at hand, at least you're available and willing, and to them you're invaluable.

"Mother I'm home!" Oh, the ego in that announcement. Oh, the glorious awareness of love. "How important I am," it seems to say, and you laugh sometimes at its brashness. But your heart is tender too, even as you realize that they take you for granted—the fact of your presence and your delight in *their* presence.

"I'm home." They rap softly on your door at night, tiptoe in.

"You can go to sleep now, Mother. I'm home." And oh, the relief of that voice, the comfort of that good night kiss, for the long vigil is ended, the hours of worrying. They're safe; the last one's in.

They grow up so fast; they go away one by one. After a while only on their visits does that glad cry come. Hectic visits, filled with their outside concerns—dates, parties, or the turmoil of families of their own. The cribs are put up, the high chairs produced, and you know that you are no longer the center and hub of their existence, no matter how joyously they proclaim their own homecoming, bursting in. Home is somewhere else. A different job, a different life, a different love to follow yours, a different person to greet them when they return.

And that once-familiar cry has taken on a new significance. It means that you don't have to watch the clock anymore when they're late. You don't have to worry. They have reached their destination. Each one is safely in. In a new and much more wonderful way, each voice is assuring you: "I'm home, Mother. I'm home!"

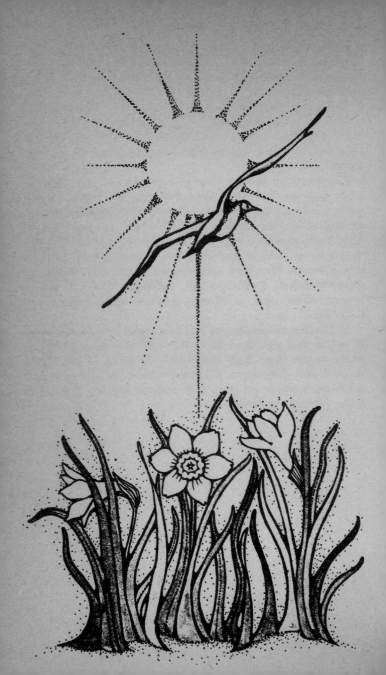

Life
    Love

Don't Let Me Take It for Granted

Lord, don't let me take this wonderful gift of life for granted.

What a miracle it is just to wake up in the morning—to be alive another day!

Just to be able to get breakfast: to crack eggs into a sizzling skillet, to pour milk for the noisy horde. Just to feel myself *functioning*—muscles and mind and voice. (A voice the rest of the family probably wishes *didn't* work quite so well!)

Remind me to stop sometimes in the midst of it—the often chaotic, maddening midst of it—and touch it, taste it, love it, feel very grateful for it. Let my heart pause to utter a little secret prayer of thanks.

Lord, don't let me postpone my appreciation until all this may be threatened. Don't let me wait for a time when I might be ill—hurt, afflicted, in traction—and out of circulation before I realize it could be taken away.

Don't let me wait till it's over—as I know one day it will be —and I look back, perhaps alone. Don't let me wait till I'm desperate, Lord. Don't let me wait till I'm dying.

Help me to be fully awake and aware of the wonders of my life *now*, while I'm healthy and agile and able. Let me appreciate it while my family is all about me, in spite of the work and the worries they cause.

Let me keep my rejoicing current. As fresh as the eggs, as new as the morning paper, as bright as my children's faces or the sunlight dancing at the door.

Thank you for each day of our life together. Don't let me take it for granted.

My Body

Thank you, God, for this body.

For the things it can feel, the things it can sense, the wondrous things it can do.

For its bright vigor at the day's beginning, for the hard sweet satisfaction of it walking, working, playing. For its very weariness at the day's end, and the dear comfort of it sleeping. Sometimes for even its pain—if only to sting me into some new awareness of my own existence upon this earth.

I look upon it sometimes in reverent amazement—for we are indeed fearfully and wonderfully made. All its secret silent machinery meshing and churning, all its muscles coordinating, the whole of it so neatly functioning.

Lord, don't let me hurt it, scar and spoil it, overindulge it or overdrive it, but don't let me coddle it either. Let me love my body enough to keep it agile and able and well, strong and clean.

Thank you that I live within this body—the real, external, forever existing me. That it has been made to serve me so happily, so well, so long. And until the day comes when I'll have no further need of it, let me appreciate it to the fullest and be grateful for it: my body.

Spring Wind

Your spring wind, Lord, is a bullying boy.

It snatches the clothes I am trying to pin on the line and whips them about my face.

It grabs the lids of trash barrels and sends them spinning like silver hoops.

It yanks the vines like a little girl's braids.

It shakes the blossom-laden trees, and the sweet confetti of their petals rains down upon me.

Your white clouds rush headlong before it. Your great trees bow and sway. Your flowers bend to its caprice.

The wind is a rollicking peddler, crying his wonderful wares, browbeating the world to buy.

I love your spring wind, Lord.

Its bright prancing. It makes me want to dance too, to roll a hoop, throw confetti, gather armloads of flowers (instead of clothes).

Your vigor is in it. Your joy is in it. Your infinite lively artistry is in it.

Thank you for spring wind, Lord.

The Ladder of Stars

On some nights the stars are simply there, brightly scattered. Distant, serenely shining, to be enjoyed but not remarked. Yet going to bed in the cool of a sweet spring night, what is it about the sky? Some feeling of expectancy, some secret withheld.

"Don't draw the shades," it seems to advise. "Don't shut out even an inch of this quiet, calmly shining night."

And so you fall asleep with the draperies still parted, and dream and rouse and dream again that the stars have come down to stand beside your bed. That somewhere near, almost near enough to climb, there rises a ladder of stars.

And you wake and sit upright . . . for there it is! Just beyond the windows and across the stream . . . The sky has sought and found some secret source of stars. Little stars in a mad multiplication, and big ones—enormous flowerings. From somewhere in the heavens they are bursting, gay little storms of unsuspected stars.

And the stars have come down, have indeed come down, and scurried about and rearranged themselves to stand at the stream's very edge. Or to hover just above it, while a few more keep fiery guard above the trees. They have become a ladder of diamonds, winking and beckoning.

All you have to do is to throw off the covers and fly off the balcony to grip their rungs. It must lead straight to heaven . . . surely you could climb it straight to heaven, this fire escape of stars.

"Garden's Up!"

The other day I saw a cartoon in which a little girl in a market was tugging at her mother's sleeve and exclaiming, "Look, Mommy—vegetables you don't have to defrost!"

I laughed, but it also gave me a pang. I grieve for children who grow up missing gardens: the springtime thrill of spying in the dark earth the first pinstripe of green that signals "seeds are up!"; the Halloween glory of lugging their own pumpkins in from among the cornstalks; most of all, the long, luxuriant feasts of the summer in between.

Nowadays, even in my small Iowa hometown, patios have replaced the potato patch, and supermarkets boom where the old orchard used to be. Here and there, like some wistful monument to the past, an iron pump still stands. But its slender arm that you used to yank so vigorously to wash the garden stuff is rusted fast. Vines claim the pump shaft—or a housewife has decoratively enshrined its feet in petunias.

When I was growing up, the garden was as much a part of a child's world as his mother's apron—a kind of character symbol. The bigger and neater it was, the more worthy of respect. To have a little, scrabbly, half-hearted garden, or a big, unkempt one, was to be labeled shiftless. And not to have a garden at all—well! You were either so impressively rich you could afford to buy from others, or so downright lazy you were probably on relief.

Gardeners, whatever their era or locale, are of-the-earth earthy. They garden out of love. Such was my Grandpa Griffith. His garden was his passion and his pride, neat as a

Grant Wood painting, its products blue-ribbon winners at the county fair. So, since Mother did not inherit his earthy fervors and Dad was a traveling salesman, it was generally Grandpa who saved the family honor by lining up Nate Mitchell and his horse, Daisy, to plow our back yard.

As Nate bellowed, "Gee-yaaap!" or "H'yaaar!" and Daisy began her jingling journey, the soil that rolled and billowed so magically from beneath the great silver blades was pitch-black. We darted behind, stamping its chocolaty richness under our feet, crumbling its clods in our hands (or throwing them at each other).

When the entire back lot had been transformed into a black and stormy sea, and we'd all had a turn at petting Daisy (the velvety prickle of her nose, her sweaty, sour-sweet flanks, still shaggy with their winter coat), the real business of gardening would begin. Dad always managed to be home for this event. Plotting and conferring as to where to put what, he and Mother would drive the stakes and stretch the cords, chalk-white against the black, so that the rows would be straight. Meanwhile, all of us clamored, "What can *I* do? Let *me* help! I want *this* corner. . . . No, that's *mine*. Mama *promised* me!"

They were remarkably patient with us. Dad, balding young, chewing gum in his chipper way, would be both funny and tender as he adjudicated claims, guided wobbly hoes, and squatted to help eager fingers shake seeds into trenches.

Then, after days of anxious watching, the miracle occurred. You rushed out one morning to discover a few beady trails of green. "Garden's up!" First, the round pushy radish leaves; then the tiny points of onions, followed by a delicate dance of lettuce sifting through. Astoundingly soon, Mother was sending us out to see if anything was big enough.

Each day we were learning a lesson no child of the super-market can appreciate: that nature, for all her bounty, gives you nothing scot-free. Soon we were being ordered forth to keep the weeds at bay. Or to chase off the rabbits, little hide-and-seek enemies that you couldn't hate even when they sheared off an entire row of your very best broccoli. And though we fretted and fussed about aching backs and blisters, we found the garden a humming, pungently sweet and tantalizing place.

The peas had an air of precious superiority, their tendrils winding gracefully up the props and clinging with delicate fingers, their blossoms like tiny white bows. Then the green pods formed, at first flat as a girl's bosom, but swelling, ripening against the day when you would descend, banging a pan, to find the pods had become long and fat, some full to bursting.

Sitting on sunny back steps, you shelled them. Birds sang, mothers worked in kitchens, screen doors banged. There was the crisp snapping of the pods. With a sensation vaguely sensuous, your fingers rooted out the emeralds they contained. Some you ate raw—juicy, flat, faintly sweet. The pods piled up on a newspaper, like the wreckage of mighty fleets. You saved a few for little boats and sailed them later across a puddle or a big tin tub.

Potatoes were a lustier vegetable, and Grandpa used a pitchfork to dig them. I can see him yet, tall and handsome and white-mustached, the clods raining softly through his lifted tines, a few potatoes clinging to the parent root like small gnomes. The rest were buried treasure scattered about, and you hunted them as you hunted eggs. These first little new potatoes had skin so fragile it could be scrubbed off with a stiff brush. The flesh underneath was rosy, like that of children whose mother has scrubbed their faces.

Sweet corn was royal fare. It grew tall and stately, hobnobbing with the hollyhocks and sunflowers. On hot nights you could sometimes hear it crackling as it stretched its joints toward the stars. We watched its development with hungry eyes, measuring our own growth against it, standing on tiptoe sometimes to pull aside the rosy silks and test the kernels with a fingernail. When the ears were ready they spurted milk, and off you streaked with the news. In blissful suspense you waited while Father or Grandfather came to check; and what joy when he broke the ear free, stripped the husks aside and waved the nude ear aloft like some triumphant offering. "Sweet corn for supper!"

Almost everything that could be eaten raw rated high with us: carrots wrenched out of the ground, orange and crisp, and washed under the pump; turnips so white and purple they looked like painted clowns; muskmelon (or cantaloupe) split open with a jackknife, the seeds scooped out, the sweet, pale flesh engorged clear down to the lime-green rind.

But nothing could surpass a tomato picked and eaten, still sun-hot, on a drowsy summer's afternoon. And no fragrance is more pungent than that of tomato vines when you brush against them in the dusk playing run-sheep-run. You gathered the scarlet globes into bushel baskets and lugged them into the kitchen. A big fire would be burning, and on the back of the stove Mason jars would be clicking and whispering like a crowd of gossips. Dad would tighten the jars at night when he was home, while Mother took proud inventory: "Fifteen quarts of tomato sauce, nine jars of catsup and five pints of piccalilli!" As this provender joined the glassy ranks that marched across our dampish, moldy-smelling cellar shelves, a feeling of peace and plenty would overtake us: a snug and squirrel-like sense of conquest and provision against the winter's cold.

Vegetables weren't all that made summer such a halcyon time. There was the fruit, as well, which progressed through tantalizing stages to clot the fences, burden the trees and rain in wanton plenty upon the ground. And we children were greedily in tune to every stage: "There's cherries big as acorns on the tree!" "The apples are getting ripe!" While parents admonished, "Not yet—it'll be another week at least. Now you kids be careful. Remember how sick you got last year."

We ate our way through summer. No competition from Good Humor men, no adult voices urging, "Now eat your vegetables, get your vitamins." Blissfully unaware, we gorged ourselves on nature's raw, fresh offerings and were as healthy as colts. When there was a pump handy we washed our plunder. If not, we ate it anyhow. ("You've got to eat a peck of dirt before you die.") There was little danger, for nobody sprayed against rivals then. Just as we didn't begrudge the bees their honey, we didn't begrudge a few apples to the worms. If we found an intruder, biting down, we simply threw the fruit away, and reached for more. . . .

I dream sometimes of those abundant summers in memory's lost emerald land of Oz. I wish my children could make little boats out of new-picked pods, and eat green apples, and raid a melon patch. I want them to know that fruits and vegetables don't grow on supermarket shelves, to be had solely for money and the opening of packages. That somewhere fruits and vegetables are being born and harvested by human hands out of God's own earth and sky and sun and rain.

A Song of Praise for Spring

This is just a little song of praise for spring, Lord, and the wonders it works in me. The way it makes me want to rearrange things, clean and decorate things—the house, the garden, myself!

It's as if your sunshine, spilling across the waking earth, spills through a woman's spirits too. Why else should I feel this mad urge to paint the bathroom (forsythia yellow), tidy up closets and cupboards, add more purple cushions of creeping phlox to the driveway?

There's a touch of April, Lord, in the lift all this bestows. To see shelves lined with gay new paper, canned goods in neat array, shoes submissive on their racks, garments weeded as neatly as the first daffodils.

I'm even inspired to "houseclean" in the manner of our mothers. Literally strip a room down to its bare branches and scrub it until it squeaks and gives off a tang as exhilarating as rain on little new leaves. Then haul (or browbeat men into hauling) furniture back—but all in new places so as to be surprised each time we sail in . . .

Or to get clothes in shape. Fix zippers, alter skirts, add or subtract belt, buckle or bow. Or to make the sewing machine sing into the night; or come home from shopping with a sense of beauty and bargains that make me feel in style with the shining new wardrobe of the world.

Best of all, Lord, spring inspires me to do some neglected housecleaning and refurbishing of my spirit.

Out with self-pity, old grudges, regrets. In with self-esteem
. . . To refresh my own interior with a new supply of forgiveness and understanding, of goals and delights and dreams.
To scatter these like seeds in the soil of myself and literally
feel them grow.

Thank you, Lord, for all these sources of sunshine for a
woman—all these ways to feel and celebrate spring.

Heart Friends

How generous is God that he has given me these few and special women who are the true friends of my heart.

How he must love me that he has let us find each other upon this crowded earth.

We are drawn to each other as if by some mystical force. We recognize each other at once. We are sisters of the spirit, who understand each other instinctively.

There is no blood between us, no common family history. Yet there are no barriers of background, or even age. Older, younger, richer, poorer—no matter. We speak the same language, we have come together in a special moment of time, and the sense of union we feel will last throughout eternity.

How generous is God that he has given me so many other women I can call friends. Dear, good, life-enriching women who add flavor, value, delight. I would be the poorer without them.

Yet surely the Lord's true concern for us, his children, is to lead us to these rare and special few. The ones who call out to us from the crowds, who hold fast to us through trials, triumphs, long separations.

The friends with whom the heart feels joyfully at home.

The Generous Artistry

How generous is your artistry, God, that you made all things in creation to be enhanced by other things.

Leaves—how lovely in themselves.

How marvelous that they sprout like tiny parasols in the sweet spring air, are opened by the heat of summer, and turned from green to crimson and gold by the tangy chemistry of fall. But no, that is not enough. You have added the sun and the wind and the rain to toss them about, adorn them with bangles, make them dance and shimmer.

And the trunks of trees.

How stately they rise, strong and sufficient with their rough dark bark. They reach for the sky, making a mighty harmony of their own. Yet their beauty too must be heightened, given an added dimension by the silver brush strokes of sun and rain.

And the rain itself.

It is not just falling water to quench the thirst of the earth. It too is enhanced by all it touches—rooftops or leaves or lake. It runs across the water before the wind like an advancing army, shields flashing. Or it falls gracefully, each drop a dancer spreading her skirts on the shining surface of a ballroom floor.

Your rocks would not need to be embellished, God.

Their gray-white stolidity, often glittering from their own white substance . . . their pure raw sculpturing. Yet even a rock is endlessly resculptured in sun and shadow and storm.

Or a mantle of moss is tossed across its shoulders, or a meandering vine. Or flowers creep from a crevice. Or a bird's nest is tucked there, from which music spurts, and brisk bright wings.

For creatures too participate in this constant interplay of loveliness.

Dogs and cats and butterflies. Squirrels and people and children and all wild things. Life . . . life . . . all dipping and darting about together, or only just pausing to observe. But all adding myriad varieties of radiance and color.

How marvelous, this ever-changing pattern of the world's beauty, God. How you must love us to create for us such interlocking loveliness.

Don't let us ever be indifferent to it. Let us always see in it your generosity, your tremendous artistry.

The Refrigerator

Oh, God, how I dread cleaning the refrigerator. And I mean that not as an oath, but a prayer.

There it stands, singing away so faithfully, keeping our foods fresh for us. Reluctantly I open it, and instead of being grateful for its overflowing plenty, I want to back away and slam the door.

Instead, let me pause a moment and thank you. How generously you provide for us. We are never hungry. There is more than enough to go around—there are even leftovers.

Leftovers. A nuisance, yes, but also a symbol of your bounty. Quite literally our cups "runneth over."

And these cups, Lord. These chill bright bowls. Thank you for them and for all the foods they hold. What an infinite variety of things are here to please and nourish us. The eggs, so delicate and white in my hands. The milk, rich and heavy in its cartons. The bins of vegetables and fruit. The tangy globes of oranges, the moist green lettuce, the red meats, and yellow cheeses.

Everything that we need to survive you quietly put upon this earth for us, and the proof is here before me. Here on these crowded shelves.

Lord, forgive me for even a moment of irritation. Flood me with thankfulness.

Bless these shelves that I scrub and restore to order. Bless my hands as I work. And bless this task; make it no longer a source of dread, but a humble form, of woman's worship—cleaning the refrigerator.

Mornings Are Special

My mother always loved the morning.

I know a lot of people do. But with her morning was special. I can't say that she never woke up cross or troubled, I'm sure she often did. But what I remember most are those mornings when she was so full of hope and joy and enthusiasm, bubbling with bright plans for the day.

"Get up," she would call from the foot of the stairs. "Oh, do get up now, come on—it's such a beautiful day!"

And as we burrowed deeper, she would launch into a veritable paean of description: "The sun is shining so brightly and the birds are singing. Just listen to them, I can hear a mockingbird. And there's a nest of orioles in the lilac bushes, there goes one now!"

She would then produce more practical reasons: "I'm going to bake and clean and that garden needs weeding, so come on, you can help, I need you. But really it's so lovely out it'll be a pleasure, a person can accomplish so much on a beautiful day!"

By noon her enthusiasm had begun to wane, by midafternoon her hopes and energies were definitely dragging. No doubt her offspring's failing to share her zest to get up and enjoy the world (and its jobs) had a lot to do with this. But she was definitely what would today be labeled "A Morning Person."

And so am I. Morning is so new, unshabby and unsoiled. Morning is like a brand-new garment fresh out of the box. You want to try it on. To wear it! No matter what its color—sunny or gray—garbed in morning nothing seems impossible.

By afternoon you're used to it, the day seems adequate, it covers you, but is no longer exciting.

By evening you're tired; the day's score is being tallied up, and sometimes you're not sure it was worth it. What did you accomplish? Nothing. Or seldom as much as you intended to. Sometimes you shrink back in dismay from the errors you have made, the miseries endured. (How could morning have so betrayed you—morning with its promise!)

Or if the promises have been fulfilled—your achievements please you, there has been excitement, unexpected pleasure— then, yes, evening can be lovely, looking back on it. But it's over when you go to bed. There's no calling back the day— the bad of it to be somehow changed, or the good of it either.

For morning people it is only in the morning that life is so entirely yours, unused, unspoiled, filled with the thrilling mystery of what lies ahead; and yet that is, right now, this moment, so beautiful, so intensely satisfying.

For me heaven will be like that. And when a voice calls, "Get up now, come on, it's morning!" I won't mind a bit.

Unexpected Company

They'll be here soon, the company I wasn't expecting and really don't want very much—but thank you for them.

Bless this house (and help me to get it cleaned up in time). This kitchen (and help me to find in it something worthy of guests).

Bless my dear foolish husband who invited them, and me as I strive to be a good hostess and a good wife to him.

Bless this table that I'm preparing; these linens (thank you that they're clean); this china and silver, these candles, wobbly though they are. This room, this meal—may it all turn out to be shining and good and lovely, to compensate for my sense of distress, ill humor, of not wanting to bother.

Oh, Lord, thank you for these guests as they drive toward us (and make them drive slowly, please).

I send out thoughts of love toward them, I send out welcome, and these thoughts ease my nervousness and make me genuinely glad inside.

Thank you for their friendship. Thank you that they have called us and can come. Thank you for the greetings and the news and the ideas that we will exchange.

Fill us all with rejoicing. Make us feel your presence among us. Bless our coming together in the warm hospitality of my house.

Moon Shadows

The moon will not let you sleep. It is huge and brightly burning. Round, intense, it pours its white fire upon all the hushed yet night-singing earth. . . .

It powders the outlines of the trees in the distance so that they melt into ghostly shapes. Yet those that branch across the window are etched by its silver tools into blackest clarity. . . .

It trembles upon the black satin surface of the lake. It pours into the room. And the beams across the ceiling are repeated in shadows drawn by the moon. . . .

Across these double lines lean the dark shadows of the window frames, making soft shifting plaids. And mounting these crossed ladders of shadow are a host of shadow figures; dark trembling shapes that march as mysteriously as spirits on some eternal journey—washing, leaning, trembling against each other. Overlapping, never still. . . .

At first you cannot imagine their source. The leaves outside? But no, the leaves are still. And then gazing down, down, you see the moon reprinted upon water that shifts, trembles, glances in its light. . . . The figures that walk your walls by moonlight are water shadows!

Scrubbing a Floor

Thank you for the privilege of scrubbing this floor.

Thank you for the health and the strength to do it. That my back is straight and my hands are whole.

I can push the mop. I can feel the hard surface under my knees when I kneel.

I can grasp the brush and let my energy flow down into it as I erase the dirt and make this floor bright and clean.

If I were blind I couldn't see the soil or the patterns of the tile or the slippery circles shining.

If I were deaf I couldn't hear the homely cheerful sounds of suds in the bucket, the crisp little whisper of brush or mop.

I would miss the music of doors banging and children shouting and the steps of people coming to walk across this bright expanse of floor.

Lord, thank you for everything that has to do with scrubbing this floor.

Bless the soap and the bucket and the brush and the hands that do it. Bless the feet that are running in right now to track it. This I accept, and thank you for.

Those feet are the reason I do it. They are the living reasons for my kneeling here—half to do a job, half in prayer.

A floor is a foundation. A family is a foundation. You are our foundation.

Bless us all, and our newly scrubbed floor.

The Runaway Canoe

You regard it rocking lightly at the dock, the just-patched and repainted family canoe.

And you feel you simply must assert yourself, if only for the children's future memories. What if they had to recall, "My mother was a hopeless nincompoop. She couldn't even paddle a canoe."

"Come, dear, how'd you like to take a ride?" you invite the littlest, doubtfully.

"You really mean it? Oh, goody, you gonna drive the boat?"

"No, let's not get too ambitious—I'm going to drive the canoe. And put on your lifejacket," you add nervously.

She scrambles eagerly in, grabs a paddle. "Can I help steer?"

"Well, maybe, after I get used to it."

You too step gingerly into the now drunkenly rocking shell, and ease down onto a cushion. "Well—" cheerily, "here we go!"

Fortified by vague recollections of having helped boyfriends paddle canoes in college, you shove off valiantly. But something seems to be wrong. Instead of heading sensibly toward the island, it rears and roots.

"Saaay, lookit Mother!" Your husband hollers from the shore: "You're sitting in the wrong end, honey."

"What difference does that make?" you demand, faintly irked.

"A lot if you expect to get anywhere. Boys, go help her," he orders. And now all the swimmers are regarding your plight and yelling instructions. To your consternation, a little crowd comes sloshing out to hold the craft steady while you stagger to the proper end.

"Go away, go away!" you order angrily as they stand by in an interested huddle. "I can do it."

"Sure you can," your husband says. "Don't watch her. You kids go on and play."

Self-consciously you keep stabbing at the water. "We'll head over to the islands," you inform your passenger confidently.

But the vessel has a stubborn will of its own. Whenever you gee it seems to buck and haw. "I tell you what—" you announce, as the island backs farther away by the minute—"let's go over to the fishing hole instead."

"Okay, I'll help." Your daughter pokes happily at the amiably nibbling waves. With growing confidence you bounce and struggle toward the sufficiently indefinite spot on the silvery platter.

Then a shrill whistle from shore. "Telephone, honey. You're wanted on the phone."

"Okay, I'll turn around, I'll be right there."

But the more fervently you lash the water, the more earnestly the vessel turns its snout toward the opposite bank and dedicates itself to the cause of taking you there.

"Hey, we live over this way, remember?"

"I know, smarty, I know, but it won't *cooperate*."

"Stick your paddle way out and pull back—"

"Turn it a little as you stroke—" "Try the opposite side—" Everybody wants to get into the act. Calling directions, the kids streak down the sand. And somebody suggests brightly, "Get out and shove."

Thoroughly flustered now and mad at the whole bunch, you try to do everything they say, only to find yourself tacking more wildly toward the wrong bank.

"Lassie, come home." A witty neighbor has joined the rousing little group.

"Oh, go drown yourself," you mutter. He's the least of your

worries, however. For now, to your horror, you realize you are about to be cast up on the lap of total strangers having a cocktail party.

They look up from their float at all the commotion, and even your little girl inquires in troubled tones, "Mother, where we *going?* Do we know those people?"

"We're about to," you sputter, through set teeth. "I—seem to have lost the hang of it," you announce in what you hope are charmingly helpless tones.

"Here, let me help." A handsome male squats on the dock, holds out a hand. "We're neighbors? Won't you join us?"

"Heeeey!" Bewildered shouts still echo from the opposite bank. "What's the big idea? Where you going? Hey, telephone!"

This House to Keep

Sometimes my home just seems so cozy, God. For no special reason it suddenly seems warm and dear—as if it had put sheltering arms around me. I feel snug, protected, like a mole deep in its burrow, or a bird in its nest.

This kitchen with its clutter . . . This bedroom with its tumbled beds . . . The family room, deserted now but warm with the memories of last night's music, last night's fire.

I feel shielded by these walls, and yet in charge. So joyfully in charge. They are mine, to do with what I please. I want to spread my wings, to draw them a little closer to my heart.

Deep instincts stir. Half-buried recollections . . .

Of childhood playhouses of the past . . . In a garage. Under the attic eaves. Or down in the ravine, with tall ferns for curtains, and fallen logs and rocks for furnishings. How snug and secret it felt and yet how free, especially when raindrops spattered overhead.

You know, Lord, how often I hate this house. Mourn its defects, deplore its confusion, want to flee its confining walls. Yet on some days love rises up to compensate—like the guilty, almost overpowering love I feel when I've been cross or unfair to the children. I want to hug it as I do them, to wash its face, straighten its clothes, tuck it in. To make it as clean and sweet and charming as I possibly can.

Because it's a part of my life, even as they are. It echoes my tastes, reflects my character, and for all its imperfections, it is warm and dear to me.

Thank you, Lord, that I have this house to keep.

The Buffet Drawer

Here's to that great repository of American living, the buffet drawer!

Even if you eat at a breakfast nook or a coffee bar in the kitchen, you must pass it, usually, on your countless travels throughout the house. And as you do so it awaits you, silent-mouthed but ever ready to open and gulp the flotsam and jetsam that nobody knows quite what to do with:

The door keys. The Charge-a-Plate. The school papers, the safety pins, the bargain soap coupons. The pencils, the notices, the pamphlets that nobody reads but somebody might want to, so you'd better not throw them out.

What housewife is so equipped with will power that, dizzily viewing the constant accumulation, she doesn't shut her eyes and simply scoop it into the blind relief of the buffet drawer?

What female is so firm in her demands that she can enforce a more orderly disposal of possessions upon her progeny? "These are your ball and jacks, take them to *your own room!*" . . . "This is your party invitation, put it where you can find it, for goodness sake." Thus though we chant in a kind of dutiful recitative day in and day out, who heeds, pray tell? Who obeys?

No, there exists a kind of common understanding: If you don't need it but want to keep it, where more safely can it go on deposit than in the buffet drawer? We even answer all inquiries thus ourselves: "Where can you find some bobby pins? Look in the buffet drawer." . . . "Has anybody seen your Scout knife? It's probably in the buffet drawer."

And even if the missing object isn't at once unearthed, how often other treasures are: "Hey, here's that cowboy wallet Grandma gave me for Christmas two years ago." . . . "I only scared up three bobby pins, but I found this jeweled barrette and this rabbit's foot and it's already brought me luck—look, here's a movie pass and it's not even dated and there's a neat matinee this afternoon."

Betimes, of course, you clean it. When it reaches the point of sheer satiety. When its jaws are so bulging full they're beginning to show leakage and you can scarcely shut them. In a burst of reform you dump the entire contents on the dining room table and sort. The tacks, the lipsticks, the buttons, the jewelry—each in its proper heap to be tidily distributed or filed away in boxes and jars. A lot of the papers can be burned —the notices of a citizens' meeting four months ago, the homework; yea, though you feel guilty twinges, those unredeemed soap coupons.

My heavens, how bare it is. How neatly compartmentalized, you gloat. This section for school tickets and such. This for the circulars. This one for combs. "And there's simply *no excuse* for its getting into such a mess again," you lecture with fervor and hope. In fact it's so clean it intimidates you. For a little while you actually refrain from the daily sweep yourself.

But soon—just when one cannot say—you too know the sweet relief of its all-embracing vaults. Of answering the inevitable, "What'll I do with this?" by the equally inevitable, "Well, for now—put it in the buffet drawer." And the queries, "Where can I find it?" with that comfortable, dependable prediction: "You know very well where it probably is—the buffet drawer!"

What Is a Cat?

A cat is first of all a kitten, to be cuddled and adored. Kittens have baby-blue eyes and plaintive, comical little mews. They have to be mopped up after and trained. Their tiny tongues lap milk like pink flags flying. They chase balls or string or their own tails, in fact anything that moves.

Kittens are gay and tender and funny and charming.

But kittens grow up to be cats.

Now their eyes have turned a bland, enigmatic green. A cat gazes directly at you, with something profound and superior in its eyes. A cat's gaze is as ancient and secretive as the sphinx.

And the things cats chase now are alive! Mice or chipmunks or bunny rabbits or birds. At this point cats cause awful conflict in the bosom of any owner. "Hooray, go after the mice!" we encourage the helpful hunter. But we want Cat to spare the birds and the little wild furred things. "You bad, you wicked creatures!" we scold, regarding the offering that Cat has proudly deposited at our feet.

Chasing the bewildered villain away, we try to mend the victim, or feeling guilty, bury it tenderly. Yet reason informs us that this is Cat's nature. No amount of punishment or protest can alter the instinctive machinery that makes him a predator. How sad, how strange.

Cats also have strange and noisy courtship customs.

Males fight, and females move constantly from litters to lovers. Even trotting them to the vets seems to make no difference to courting Toms. They still come caterwauling under windows, with noises that put a banshee or a colicky baby to shame.

Cats also enjoy a good snooze in unlikely places—the buffet, a dresser drawer, a closet shelf, your husband's hat. They enjoy sharpening claws on the furniture, and kneading them on anything soft and woolly, such as blankets or your best sweaters.

A good way to lure them from the sofa is by providing them with a scratching board covered with burlap and baited with a dash of catnip. (For some reason they go mad when they sniff catnip, rolling and squirming as if intoxicated. It is the cat's LSD.)

Cats *don't* suck baby's breath, as is maliciously rumored; but they are curious about anything that moves, attracted by the smell of milk and softness, so they can wake him up and disturb him. Ernest Hemingway says, in *A Moveable Feast,* that during those early Paris years their cat, F. Puss, served as their son's baby sitter.

Cats are very loving. They will wind between your legs when you are trying to get dinner on the table. They will plop on your lap when you're reading or sewing, and want to cuddle. Their purring is steady, insistent, and as comforting as a kettle boiling joyously on the hearth.

Cats, like people, have personality. Some are gentle, some gay, some solemn, some bold, some are cowards. All are a nuisance. And we bother with them for simply one reason: We love them!

Morning Birds

How impudent are morning birds! How annoyingly gay. Tired, needing sleep, you hear them starting up sometimes outside your window, like insistent little alarm clocks that you can't shut off or hurl away. Trilling and cheeping and shrilling their glad little cries. Running scales. Ringing bells of brightness. Chiming.

How they carry on, unaware of the head that plunges into the pillow. Or the being who rises, stalks to the window, prepared to shoo or shout "Oh, go away!"

Only you cannot. No, you cannot. For the day itself is too giddily joyful too. Fresh, untasted. New and sparkling. The sky a cool pink-tinged blue.

The trees are all atwinkle in the coming sun. Their branches dip slightly under the fragile singers. Leaves tremble as, with a spurt of wings, a glimmer of color, an oriole or a cardinal soars away.

By contrast—how silently. How effortless the lift of wings. How totally unresistant. Their motion is like the spontaneous spill of music from their throats. Birds are so relaxed. They sound and seem so free, so happy, because they don't fight their surroundings. They simply flow into them.

And now you think: How peaceful are morning birds. How restful.

For their joy is contagious. You feel it beginning to dance and sparkle within you as your own resistance gives way. You want to laugh. You want to join their bright chorus and go singing into the new day.

Oh, but you're not a bird, remember? The day will be complex. Filled with phone calls, duties, problems, jobs that nobody, man, or bird, could effortlessly fly through. But maybe the birds have been little emissaries to prepare you. "Sing if you can" they may have been saying. "But when you can't, remember our silence too."

Fortify Me with Memories

Sometimes life seems almost too wonderful, Lord.

My husband's arms around me. A new baby kitten-soft on my shoulder. A son who (after all that trouble) is turning into a bright and handsome boy. A daughter who's witty and lovely. A new puppy to be gathered around and adored.

Friends calling their good nights after an unusually happy party. A moment of rare understanding with another friend on the phone. An hour of high excitement when the mailman brings wonderful news.

There are times when all these things seem to shout and sing within me, Lord. To merge into something almost too beautiful, like a sunset or a symphony. Fused into some instant or hour of perfection. At times I can scarcely bear it, Lord—this beauty, this benediction.

Oh, help me to remember it, please . . .

When the baby screams all night with the colic. When the pup throws up on the kitchen floor. When my husband is cross and discouraged. When the son fails me and the daughter becomes a blind fury against me.

Gird me with the shining moments, God. Fortify me with memories.

Help me to realize during the pain and the petulance and the anguish that life *is* truly wonderful, Lord. And it takes the grim moments to enhance the ecstasy.

The Angel Bird

Each year the herons come—stately steel-blue beings who nest in the rushes across from the cabin, and stalk the fishes on slender legs. They fly with their long necks arched inward, emitting their curious cry, "Frahnk, frahnk!"

There is always mystery and excitement about any large bird. These almost people-sized creatures who can lift themselves so magically and soar off into the sky. As if they could carry you with them if you made your longing clear and they so willed.

Then there are the bitterns, a chunkier smaller species, the brown of the weeds. But loveliest of all the herons is the white one which descends once a season, like a visiting celebrity, and usually alone.

"Mommy, guess what? An angel flew by my window this morning!" a child exclaims. And so it seems. For there is something unearthly about that white span of wings against the vivid blue sky. Something that speaks of purity, joy and peace, coasting down.

How placidly it perches upon the piece of driftwood it has chosen; the silver of the sun-bleached wood, the snowy body, a statue reflected on the water. How patiently it stands in the shallows, or walks the sands with slow elegant grace. It is oblivious to our admiring gaze. Yet sometimes the children are convinced it dips its wings to us, going by. And sometimes it cuts so close to the cabin you could reach out and touch it, so it seems.

You know better. It would be like trying to touch an angel.

It would be like holding in your hands for one brief, enthralling instant the bright bird of happiness. It would be too much.

But whenever anyone announces its arrival, or calls out, "The white heron's still here," it is like a good omen. You feel that for a small and lovely while you have a heavenly guardian.

His Very World Dances

To me, no art form speaks more eloquently of my Creator than the dance. His very world dances! Almost everything in nature that he has made.

Look out the window, now, right now. Whatever the season, look out upon the vast living stage of the world. How hard it is for nature to be still; even on the stillest summer days the squirrels leap and scurry, the streams cavort, ballets of tiny butterflies dip and swirl. And when the wind stirs—! Even now, November—a chill bright golden day. The grass has nearly lost its green, the trees are almost bare. Yet lean and stripped, those trees lift their arms to the sky as if in worship, and dance. The few remaining leaves do a happy roundelay as they come skirling down. They are little girls in dancing class, skittering this way and that. They skip across my window as I write, land briefly, pirouette on.

Below is the water, sequin-skirted in the sun. Moving, ever-moving to the cadences of its currents and the wind. The waves keep time. Like a perfectly trained chorus, a line of them swings forward arm in arm, white-plumed; bowing their heads in unison they break, rise, surge shoreward, regroup. There with another little bow they disperse, reach toward me, then retreat to dance again.

Soon winter will stop their performance, polish the stage. But then the snows will come dancing down, weaving and twining like Maypole streamers as they fall. . . . Then spring and the triumphal melting, the dancing of rain, the dance of buds on the boughs and petals on the breeze.

Lord, how you must love dancing to put its rhythms into all these things. And into your creatures—insect, bird or beast. To equip them with such grace.

More Stately Mansions

"Build thee more stately mansions, O my soul!"—Another of Mother's favorite quotations. From *The Chambered Nautilus*, by Oliver Wendell Holmes . . . She looks up from the washboard with a twinkle in her eyes, tosses back a lock of her long dark hair, and goes on, as her hands wring out the clothes: "As the swift seasons roll! Leave thy low-vaulted past!"

Oh, Mom, that little house where you worked so hard! . . . You could have held your own in any stately mansion, and you set foot in so few during your life. But then why should you? you already occupied so many. Mansions of the spirit, mansions of the mind. The Lord had given you the keys, and you wandered them at will. . . . Through books—of poetry, especially. Through the music you listened to with such pleasure ironing, baking, keeping your family clean. Through copies of famous paintings cut so carefully from magazines.

It was years before you saw the originals of some of those paintings in the galleries. How awed and astonished you were at their size. A gigantic Rubens, I remember, claiming half a wall—though it had hung cozily in its dime-store frame over your bed and Dad's for years. You gasp, then giggle behind your hand—"Suppose Rubens ever dreamed he'd hang in *our* stately mansion?"

Stately mansions . . . the cold marble floors ring beneath our heels as we walk them, Mother and I, under the vaulted ceilings. The flowers are bright in the courtyards, the fountains sing and splash. We wander from picture to picture, sitting often to rest, for she's getting old now and her feet hurt and she has to get her breath. . . . We sit loving the place, its sculpture, its brasses and bronzes and tiles. Then we rise and find the oriental wing. . . . How she loves the Chinese porcelains. Getting her big round reading glass from her bag, she studies each huge vase or urn carefully, remarking the exquisite detail, the intricacy of design. And now she alludes to "Kubla Khan": " 'Through wood and dale the sacred river ran, Then reached the caverns measureless to man.' You know I'd have loved to have a Ming vase, but unfortunately the Jewel Tea man never gave them for premiums, and I doubt if you could get one today with trading stamps."

Even as I laugh and hug her, my heart breaks. I want, with sudden blind passion, to place her in her stately mansion surrounded by all the beautiful things her soul craves.

But later, long after she's asleep, I go outside and gaze up at the stars sparkling so brightly. And the last few lines of her *Chambered Nautilus* come to me:

> *Let each new temple, nobler than the last,*
> *Shut thee from heaven with a dome more vast,*
> *Till thou at length art free,*
> *Leaving thine outgrown shell by life's unresting sea!*

And then the words, from another source altogether: "In my Father's house are many mansions."

Mother will have her mansions.

New Year's Eve

It's almost over, Lord. The old year's almost over.

In a few minutes the whistles and bells will proclaim it. "Forget it, it's over. Off with the old, on with the new!"

But I'm already a little homesick for the old year, Lord. I don't want it to be over, not really. I want to hang onto it a little longer. The happiness it held—the joys and surprises. Big important ones, yes, but the little ones too. Delights that were often too small or perhaps too frequent even to realize, to appreciate and savor before they vanished.

Even the pain and problems—somehow I want to cling to them too. I long to rush back, reclaim them. Handle them differently, be more careful, more patient, more generous, more wise. I don't *want* the New Year, Lord. I just want another chance at the old one!

But mostly I don't want to part with it just yet. For we loved it, whatever mistakes we made. It was ours, our life together.

But now the bells are clanging, the whistles are shrieking. People are laughing and singing—and I am caught up in the excitement too. "Don't look back," everything seems to be shouting. "Look ahead!"

And a great exhilaration courses through me as I realize: Yes, yes, they are right. How wonderful, that every year you present us with this great, new, shining package of time.

How promising its contents. How mysterious. How thrilling, challenging, in some ways almost frightening. Yet mainly how marvelous—that we can discover those contents only as we live them. Until we have stripped off the final wrapping of the final day and another year lies at our feet.

Revealed, completed, endured, enjoyed. But whole at last, and so—wholly and utterly ours.

Thank you that as we put the old year away with all the tattered and treasured Years Past, you always give us a new one to open.

Life is so dear. Each year is so dear. Each *day* is so dear. Thank you for every moment, Lord.

Self
Love

Who Am I?

Oh, God, who am I? Where did I come from and where am I going? What am I doing here?

Sometimes, passing a mirror, I am startled by the stranger who seems to be wearing my face. Who is this person who looks like me (poor thing) and rushes around in my body?

She cleans up the kitchen, sorts the laundry, yells at children, loves, worries about and fights with a man who seems to be her husband.

She goes to bed at night, gets up in the morning, cooks, eats, gets other people off to their destinations and then hurries to her job. A job in a sometimes drearily familiar, sometimes startlingly strange place. Or a club where she knows almost everybody—and nobody, actually.

And we are the same person, this woman and I. Yet different, too—as if I am allowed to wake up sometimes in her presence and cry out: "Hey . . . *you!* Who are you, and what are you doing here?" And she can only regard me, stricken and surprised.

Who am I? Who am I, God?

I am alive—I must be. See, I am shaking a hand: I can feel it warm against mine. I am conducting a meeting: I hear my own voice calling for the treasurer's report. I am racing to the car, gabbling with somebody; our heels click on the walk, the door bangs. I am hurtling along a highway to pick up a child and take him to Little League.

But in the very moment of awareness, I am sometimes pierced by the sheer pointlessness of all this.

What does it matter, God? What does it *matter* whether the clothes get sorted, the kitchen cleaned, the treasurer read her dull report? What would it matter if I didn't show up for work? Would the course of human events be altered in the least if my son didn't get to the ball game?

This woman who seems to be doing these things in my body, wearing the label of my name. What has she got to do with *me?*

Forgive me if this sounds frenzied, God. I *feel* frenzied—and frightened sometimes.

It's all going by so fast. Life's rushing past me, time is sweeping me along in its torrent, and I don't know where I'm going, or why. I long to grab something along the way. I can't slow it down, but I feel that I've got to grab something, hang onto something, or I'll be obliterated altogether. The real me (if there is such a creature) will be even more lost than she is now.

Already half-deafened by the demands of other people, half-blinded, desensitized, she will go down to death with her own needs not only unmet but only half-recognized.

Rescue me, Lord. Stretch out your hand to me.

I know you must be out there—somewhere. And if I can only find you, hang onto you, perhaps I can be saved. Not in the sense of an afterlife, but saved from the choking futility of this life now.

I am groping for you, God. Stretch out your hand—and don't let me fight you away. Draw me onto a place where I can at least get perspective. Where I can meet myself on quieter terms and try to figure out who I am, where I am going—and why.

Time Out for Love

Lord, don't ever let me be too busy to love . . .

A child who comes running in for a hug and lavish exclamations of praise because he's just learned to stand on his head. Yea, though I'm trying to make bouillabaisse and to keep the clams from getting all over the kitchen and the lobsters from crawling off, don't let me shoo him away.

Don't let me be too busy to love, Lord . . .

A neighbor who's just had a fight with her husband and needs a shoulder to cry on; or who's just had her first poem published and is dying to celebrate with someone. Though I'm already behind schedule and there's company coming, don't let me be too busy to listen and, in this way, to love.

Lord, don't let me be too busy to love . . .

A son who's home unexpectedly from boot camp with a buddy who hasn't got a home to go to—both starved for some good old-fashioned fried potatoes and corn bread. No matter how hectic my day's program, don't let me be too busy to fix it (well, at least give them a hand). Above all, to show him how thrilled I am to have him back and the other kid with him.

Don't let me be to busy to love, Lord . . .

My husband when he's tired and discouraged, or high from a big deal at the office, or simply wants my attention. Don't let me be too preoccupied with TV or a book or a friend on the phone or my own day's score of frustrations and peaks and valleys to give him what he longs for. Don't let me be too busy to love.

And now, Lord, thank you for giving me so many people, so many opportunities to love. But please forgive me when I fail them; help them to forgive me, and me to forgive myself.

You made me human, and there is only so much of me to go around.

The New Outfit

Oh, Lord, dear Lord, I've spent too much on this new outfit. I'm beginning to worry even as I carry it excitedly down the street.

It's so lovely—the most becoming thing I've found in years. I felt I simply had to have it, and in one mad moment I bought it. But now the price tag is like a weight dragging at my steps. Guilt and anxiety are beginning to dim the first high delight I felt.

I see very nice looking things much more reasonable, it seems, in the windows I pass. I wince to recall what I paid, I deplore my rash impulse. I think of the bills, the budget, the things the children need.

What kind of mother am I to blow all that money on myself?

Lord, I am hesitating. Perhaps I should turn around right here before I lose my nerve and take it back! . . . Help me to do the right thing now, this minute, while the traffic light still says STOP . . . But no, it's turned to green, I'm somehow being propelled across the street, carrying my lovely box.

And my heart is suddenly lighter as a sweet conviction dawns: Anything cheaper that I didn't really *care* about would be a disappointment, not only to me but to the rest of them. They *want* me to feel and look the way I feel and look in this new outfit!

Thank you, Lord, for making me realize that now and then a woman simply has to be extravagant.

I've Said "Yes" Once Too Often

Oh, God, I've done it again, I've said "Yes" once too often and now I'm stuck with this extra job.

How will I manage to accomplish everything? All these committees, all these meetings, all these phone calls.

Right now I don't see where there'll be enough time in the day (or night). I don't see where my strength is coming from.

Only you will help me. You will give me strength. You will give me the intelligence to manage. You, who created time, will even give me that.

Now let me quietly thank you for this challenge. If I'm a fool to take on so much—all right, you, who made me so, will not leave me stranded. You will fortify, you will supply my needs.

Bless the people with whom I'll be involved. Bless the job I've undertaken, and I know it will prove worthy of the efforts I bring to it.

Self-awareness

What a wonderful thing is self-awareness. It is the touchstone of a full, vibrant, fulfilling life.

I don't mean self-consciousness in the sense that we have been warned about. A preoccupation with how you'll look and act with other people only makes anyone anxious and ill at ease. No, no, self-AWARENESS is something quite different. It is the ability to appreciate your own being. To realize even in little ways, the sheer magic of being alive.

SELF-AWARENESS is practiced constantly by children. They glory in how fast they can run, how loud they can sing. They rejoice in how they are growing, in whatever dimension . . . We adults lose this natural delight; bogged down with responsibilities and concerns for other people, we go dull and take ourselves for granted. We even begin to fret and stew and harp and complain about the burdens that are the inevitable accompaniment of life.

Yet how glorious it is just to BE here on this planet, able even to cope with and carry these trials. What a marvel simply to exist! . . . To be YOU, right now, this moment, in that body, for all its limitations, is a priceless thing, and it won't last forever. So pause and become AWARE OF IT.

Practice Being Grateful

Practice being grateful for every breath you draw. Whatever your religions or your doubts, each of us has materialized out of a mystery. But one undeniable fact is you are here, constantly breathing and tasting the most precious commodity of all—life. Rejoice in the simple act of getting out of bed in the morning, the night's sleep behind you. Let the hot and cold water of the shower pound down upon you stirring you to the awareness, "Hey, it's me!" Smell the breakfast you are cooking for yourself or other people, hear the sounds of kitchen and family and dogs and cats and cars. Be AWARE of yourself in relation to all these things, an active, vigorous participating being, vital to others—yes, but vital as well to YOU.

Look at every member of your body with wonder. Every finger, toe, elbow, knee. Breast and belly and back. How remarkable their smooth intricate joinings, what a complex package. And these eyes to see, these ears to hear . . . Don't wait until some of these senses are threatened; don't wait till you're in a hospital having a hysterectomy—in pain, in fear, in traction. Bless your body and its creator for its abilities now. Thank God—and it—your SELF—this physical vehicle of the spirit, for serving you.

It Makes You More Attractive

Self-awareness even makes you more attractive. It puts a new spring in your step, a new sparkle in your eyes. And you can't be truly self-aware and let yourself go. The truly self-aware person refuses to submit to anything that despoils his own image. It is self-awareness that makes him step on the scales, do those exercises, brush the hair until it shines. When you're in league with beauty you're in league with one of the nicest aspects of life.

Take time for self-awareness!

The Compliment

I want to suggest a new Beatitude: "Blessed are the sincere who pay compliments."

For I have just had a compliment, and it has changed my day.

I was irritated. Tired. Discouraged. Nothing seemed much use. Now suddenly all this is changed.

I feel a spurt of enthusiasm, of energy and joy. I am filled with hope. I like the whole world better, and myself, and even you.

Lord, bless the person who did this for me.

He probably hasn't the faintest idea how his few words affected me. But wherever he is, whatever he's doing, bless him. Let him too feel this sense of fulfillment, this recharge of fire and faith and joy.

Getting at It

Oh, Lord, please help me to stop worrying about this annual bazaar they've put me in charge of, and get *at* it!

You know how weak I am, and what a procrastinator. How I let myself get talked into things I sometimes later regret. How I lie awake nights dreading what I've undertaken, scared I won't be up to it. You know the times I've panicked, even considered making excuses for myself and trying to get out of it.

And the longer I put off getting started the worse it gets.

Now, with your help, this is going to stop. Not only because time's flying by and there's so much to be done, but because I'm ashamed of this self-inflicted suffering.

So here goes, God. Today, this minute, I'm getting at it. (There. The very resolution has a calming effect!)

I'm drawing up a plan of action. I'm calling committee meetings. I'm already getting ideas, exciting ones (what strange things happen once the gates are simply unlocked)!

I know it won't be easy, but you've made me realize it won't be all that hard. You will give me self-confidence and strength —and ultimate success. But you can't do any of these things for any of us until we *start*.

(Come to think of it—if you created the world and its creatures and even the universe in seven days, you must have just made up your mind and *done* it. And maybe even *you* didn't realize how great was your own potential or how vast would be the result.)

I've Got to Talk to Somebody, God

I've got to talk to somebody, God.

I'm worried, I'm unhappy. I feel inadequate so often, hopeless, defeated, afraid.

Or again I'm so filled with delight I want to run into the streets proclaiming, "Stop, world, listen! Hear this wonderful thing."

But nobody pauses to listen, out there or here—here in the very house where I live. Even those closest to me are so busy, so absorbed in their own concerns.

They nod and murmur and make an effort to share it, but they can't; I know they can't before I begin.

There are all these walls between us—husband and wife, parent and child, neighbor and neighbor, friend and friend.

Walls of self. Walls of silence. Even walls of words.

For even when we try to talk to each other new walls begin to rise. We camouflage, we hold back, we make ourselves sound better than we really are. Or we are shocked and hurt by what is revealed. Or we sit privately in judgment, criticizing even when we pretend to agree.

But with you, Lord, there are no walls.

You, who made me, know my deepest emotions, my most secret thoughts. You know the good of me and the bad of me, you already understand.

Why, then, do I turn to you?

Because as I talk to you my disappointments are eased, my

joys are enhanced. I find solutions to my problems, or the strength to endure what I must.

From your perfect understanding I receive understanding for my own life's needs.

Thank you that I can always turn to you. I've got to talk to somebody, God.

Give Me a Generous Spirit

Give me generosity of spirit, God. True generosity of spirit so that I can be truly glad, and show it, when other people succeed.

It's not hard to share a recipe or a baby sitter. Not a bit hard to lend a neighbor a tablecloth or an egg. It's even kind of thrilling to come to somebody's rescue with your best bag or prized (if unpaid for) mink.

And for most of us sympathy comes easy. To lend an ear to a friend's troubles, be a tower of strength in times of illness or disaster . . . There's a heady drama about being needed; the heart feels proud of itself, it receives more than it gives.

But oh, Lord, how much harder it is to share an hour of joy, of triumph. To be genuinely proud of somebody else. To be generous with praise . . . When another woman's child has made the Honor Society or the football team, or starred in the school play. When her husband has won a big promotion. Or when she herself has done something important, something exciting. When the flags of her life are flying!

That's the true test of friendship, Lord. Not when we feel luckier and stronger, when we can reach *down* to help somebody. But when we feel less lucky, our importance threatened; when we've got to reach *up* to give.

Guard me against jealousy, God. Free me from envy. Flood my heart with genuine joy, and help me to show it, when my friends succeed.

Bless My Good Intentions

Lord, please bless my good intentions.

I make so many promises to myself about all the nice things I'm going to do: Have somebody over. Phone, write, send books and get-well cards and flowers.

You know how often I lie awake at night planning the delights I want to do for people. Or mentally writing the most beautiful letters.

You know my heart is full of love—but also how full of other things is my day. Duties, demands, problems. So that, all too often, these other things don't get past my mental gates. Or are hopelessly blocked or detoured when they do.

The get-well cards I buy get lost—or I can't find the right address. The people I try to cheer up with a phone call are already on the phone, or out! The budget won't quite stand the strain of flowers, and there's nothing but a few scraggly marigolds in the yard.

The cake I bake for the shut-in falls, or the car won't start to take it to her. When I sit down to write those lovely letters, the lovely words have vanished—or there's a sudden immediate crisis to be resolved.

They say hell is paved with good intentions, Lord. But I wonder if the paths to heaven aren't cobbled with them too?

Surely you give us credit for our kindly thoughts. At least they're better than critical ones even when, through life's complications of our own procrastination, we fail to follow through.

You've shown us that we are more than body, we are spirit. And thoughts are powerful things. Maybe the vibrations of love they release, actually accomplish more than we know!

Anyway, Lord, please bless my good intentions.

Thank Goodness
They Still Love Us

The trees stand bare and gray. To see them now you wouldn't dream (if you hadn't seen it) that soon, in a few weeks, they will burst forth in loveliness. And that the earth, now sodden and brown, will likewise become green, and gay with flowers.

But we know that the world is just waiting . . . resting . . . It can't be beautiful all the time. It has to have these periods in which to replenish its juices. To store up, get ready for spring. And we like it anyway. We take this for granted; we forgive it . . .

And it's this way with people. We can't always be beautiful. We can't constantly go through life all dressed up. We've got to take off our makeup, get into comfortable clothes. We have periods, sometimes for days, weeks, sometimes only a few hours, when we too are drab and colorless and plain, not only in our looks but in our performance.

But those who truly care about us understand. They don't mind; they forgive us. Sometimes it only makes us more dear to them, more human in our imperfections. Thank goodness, they still love us!

Give Me Patience

Oh, God, give me patience!

With this child who's telling his eager, long-winded story. Let me keep smiling and pretending I'm enthralled. If I don't, if I cut him off he'll not only be hurt, he may not come to me with something really important next time. But, dear Lord, help me to guide him gently to the climax soon.

Oh, God, give me patience!

With this baby who's dawdling over his food. He must eat, the doctor says, and I mustn't coax, threaten, or grab him and shake him as I'm tempted to—even though I know it would only make things worse and damage us both. Help me to sit quietly waiting, waiting, learning patience.

Oh, God, give me patience!

With this boring old lady who wants me to look at all the pictures of her grandchildren and listen (again) to her oft-told tales. Help me to remember that I may be just as difficult some day, and that by showing warm interest I can add a little joy to her few remaining days. Let me love her instead of resent the time she's taking. Let me gain something from enduring this hour with her. Let me learn through her the lesson of patience.

Oh, God, give me patience—as I wait for a friend who is late, or for a line that's busy, or for traffic to clear. Let me be fully aware of my surroundings as I wait—the feel of the chair upon which I sit, the passing parade of people, or the scent and color and sound of the very air. Help me to realize that no time is really wasted in this life so long as we are fully awake to the moment, so long as we are aware.

Oh, God, give me patience—with myself!

With my follies, my hasty words, my own mistakes. The times when I seem a hopeless bumbler unworthy of friend or family or the company of any human being, so that I get into a panic and think, "Why am I taking up space on the earth? Why can't I flee, vanish into eternity, simply disappear?

Help me to stop wrestling with remorse. Taking a futile inventory. Waking up in the night to berate myself for "things I ought to have done and things I ought not to have done." Reassure me, oh God, that there *is* health and hope and goodness in me, and that if I just have patience they will take over. I'll become the person I want to be and that you expect me to.

Let Me Take Time for Beauty

Lord, let me take time for beauty.

Time for a jug of flowers on the table, or a plant if flowers aren't in bloom. Time for a dab of lipstick or a fresh blouse before the family comes home. Don't let me settle for the dingy, the shabby, the ugly—either with myself or with my house, just because I'm too lazy to make the effort.

Give me the energy and the will to provide a bit of beauty.

You've made the world so beautiful, Lord, let me take time to see it. Even as I'm rushing to the market or driving children to their destinations, let me be aware of it: the glory of hills and woods and shining water. The colors of traffic lights and yellow buses, of fruit stands and lumberyards, of girls wearing bright scarves that dance in the breeze.

Let me take time for the beauty in my own back yard, Lord.

Let me lift my eyes from the dishes to rejoice in the sunshine spilling through the trees. In the squirrels darting jaunty-plumed along the bleached boards of the fence. In the raindrops strung out on the clothesline like a string of crystal beads.

Let me take time for the children. How quick they are to discover beauty and come running to us with their offerings.

Don't let me be too busy to exclaim over these treasures: a bluejay's bright feather, the first violets and dandelions, a shell, a pretty stone. God, forgive me for the time (I wince to remember) when, involved in some dull task—ironing maybe —I shooed away a child who was begging, "Look, come look. A butterfly!" A cocoon was breaking, I learned later. He wanted me beside him to witness this miracle, this birth of beauty out of its dark cage.

Dear God, to live at all is such a miracle—whether as bug or bird or creature of any kind. To come into existence upon this planet and be able to witness its beauty is such a privilege, especially for a human being.

Help us to cherish and be a part of that beauty.

Let me take time for beauty, God.

The Courage to Be Kind

Dear Lord, give me . . . them . . . somebody the courage to be kind.

That poor man who just got on the subway is so shabby, so talkative, so obviously confused. He doesn't know where to get off, but the woman he asked just gave him a cold stare and pointedly moved away. The man on the other side of him has turned his back.

Nobody will help him, Lord, and my heart hurts. It hurts so for him, but it's pounding for me too. I don't want to be conspicuous—to have them stare coldly at *me*. But oh, Lord, I know where he wants to go, and I can't stand it any longer. Please give me the courage to lean across the aisle, force a smile and signal with my lips and my fingers: "Three more stops."

And now, oh, Lord, give me even more courage, for he has lurched over to my side. He wants to talk—talk in a loud, eager voice about the job he's going to apply for and why it's important that he get there on time.

Yes, yes, he's been drinking, and he probably won't get it, poor guy. But thank you that I'm able to listen, to offer a little encouragement and to see that he doesn't miss his stop.

Thank you for his grateful handclasp at parting, his smile from the platform, his jaunty yet wistful wave. Thank you that I no longer care what the other passengers think, because my conscience is at rest and my heart is warm.

Please help him, Lord, and bless him. And thank you for giving me the simple courage to be kind.

Don't Let Me Be So
Hard on Myself

Father, please don't let me be so impatient with myself.

I fret, I scold, I deplore my many shortcomings.

Why am I so messy? Why do I get myself into such complicated situations? Now why did I say *that*? Won't I ever learn?

My mind carries on an idiot monologue of self-reproach. Or I lie awake bewailing the day's mistakes. I wince before them. I call myself names I would never call other people. I am stung and tormented by these self-lacerations.

I know all this is useless. The more I berate myself the worse I seem to become.

And it gets between us. It is unworthy of the trust I should have in you who made me as I am, and who loves me despite my faults.

I know that you want me to be aware of them and to improve as best I can. But help me to forgive myself a little quicker, to be a little kinder to myself.

Let Me Go Gently

Let me go gently through life, Lord, so much more gently.

Right now, calm my exasperation as I try for the third time to get that telephone operator to respond. Let me sit gently, think gently, speak gently when the connection is made. (It may not be her fault. Or she may be young and new to the job . . . or older and troubled by the very same problems I have.)

Smooth my sharp edges of person and temper and tongue. Give me gentleness in dealing with people. Strangers like this, who are human too, subject to error and hurt. And gentleness with my family . . . Not softness, no—keep me firm—but gentle of voice instead of shrill. Gentle of movement and manner and touch.

When life frustrates me, delays me, I want to grab it and shake it and rush it on. Or when it comes bashing and battering at me, every impulse yells, "Fight back!" But all this is so destructive, it only wastes more time and burns up precious energy. Remind me that true strength lies in gentleness.

Help me to practice gentleness. In small inconveniences like this as well as large problems with those close to me. If I can just keep gentle, firm but gentle, then I'll be better able to meet life's major crises with dignity and strength.

Thank you for giving me gentleness, God.

"If Only"

Please rescue me, God, from the "if onlys."

If only my husband was home more, helped more, would try to be more understanding . . . If only the children would mind, cooperate, pick up after themselves, study harder, do better in school . . . If only my neighbors were more congenial . . . If only my friends were more considerate . . .

Then—ah *then* I'd be a happier person, able to be more efficient, productive, make my life really count.

Please help me to stop this blaming of outside circumstances, Lord, and start taking myself in hand.

And this includes bidding good-bye to the "if onlys" that keep beckoning me to look back:

If only I'd gone on to graduate school instead of getting married . . . If only I hadn't had my first baby so soon . . . If only I had encouraged my husband to go into business for himself . . . or *hadn't* discouraged him from buying that land (it's worth a fortune now) . . . If only . . . if only . . .

Lord, I know there's nothing more futile than these "if onlys." None of life's choices are guaranteed. The "mistake" of the past may have been a godsend in disguise. And we will never know, so how can we ever judge?

Only one thing is sure—that what we did or didn't do then, or what other people do or don't do now, has very little bearing on me. My happiness today.

So help me to shape up, Lord. To face my problems without the crutch of "if onlys" I've been leaning on.

Talking to Yourself

They say talking to yourself is a sign of being nutty. Well then I enjoy being nutty and I'd go nuttier still if, when I'm alone, I kept all my lovely words locked away. Talking to myself helps keep my life in order. I'm my own best listener and I'm company for me. I have the best time talking to myself.

I talk to the dog, the cat. I talk to my plants and I often address even such objects as the oven or the piano or my false eyelashes: "Come on now, oven, get going if that roast is to be done by seven o'clock." "Don't feel bad, dear piano, I really love you, and I promise to have you tuned next week." As for what I say to my false eyelashes, especially when they won't go on straight—well, sometimes that's better left unsaid.

The dog's tail thumps in quick response to every word. The cat cuddles up, purring, or caresses my legs. Even the plants perk up at a few kind comments; scientists have proved that, even if I could not see it for myself. As for inanimate objects— immovable, solid, mostly voiceless—how do we know they don't respond in their own way? I like to imagine the oven's heart burns a bit more brightly, and the piano has a happier plink as I run a hand affectionately along its keys. Even eyelashes seem to behave if given a little fond coaxing or scolding.

Talking to myself helps keep my life in shape. I tell myself what I've got to do each day: "First, call the bank, and then the baker and order the cake for the party. Then be sure to put those clothes in the machine before you warm up the car."

I also take oral inventory before going anywhere: "Makeup

kit, glasses, notebook, pencil, checkbook, change—and oh, yes, don't forget the slips for the cleaner's and the mail."

I frequently scold myself—especially after hanging up the phone: "What an idiot! Now why did you say THAT?"

And I praise myself, especially for deeds well done: "Gee, what a thrill to see the house looking so nice and clean. A lot of work but it was worth it, hooray for me!"

I sometimes comfort myself in secret when there's nobody else to do so: "Now don't feel bad, forget it, you did the best you could."

Thank goodness I'm not the only one who has this habit. If I were I'd think I was a little nuttier than I am. A lot of other people tell me they're unabashed self-talkers-to, too. Even if they didn't I'd guess it—just observe the lips engaged in solitary discourse in passing cars.

So if you're one of us, admit it. And welcome to the club.

Help Me to Unclutter My Life

Help me to unclutter my life, Lord.

Rescue me from this eternal confusion of belongings (mine and other people's) that just won't stay orderly. This suffocation of phone calls, clubs and committees. ("No man can serve two masters," you said. A woman is lucky if she *has* only two!) This choke of bills and papers and magazines and junk mail. I buy too many things, subscribe to too many things, belong to too many things. The result is such confusion I can't really enjoy or do justice to anything!

Deliver me from some of this, Lord. Help me to stop bewailing this clutter and work out some plan for cutting down.

Give me the will power to stop buying things we don't really need and that only become a chore to take care of. Give me more sales resistance when it comes to antique stores and white-elephant sales and supermarkets. And give, oh give me the will power to get rid of a lot of things we already have. To unclutter my cupboards and closets and attic of things hung onto too long.

And oh, Lord, help me to unclutter my life of too many activities. Give me the self-discipline to stop joining things. And to weed out the organizations that don't really matter to me. (They'll be better off without me.) And the strength to say "No!" more often when the telephone rings.

Lord, show me a way of uncluttering my life even of too many people without being unkind. A way to love and help people without letting them gobble me alive.

There are so many dear, wonderful people I long to see, need to be with for my own soul's growth. Yet we are lost to each other because of this profligate squandering of energy and time. Give me the determination to reclaim these truly life-strengthening friends, at whatever cost to other idle, meaningless relationships.

And while I'm at it, Lord, help me to unclutter my mind. Of regrets and resentments and anxieties, of idiotic dialogues and foolish broodings. Sweep it clean and free. Make it calm and quiet. Make it orderly.

Put me in control of it as well as my house . . . and my calendar . . . and my harried spirit. Thank you. With your help I know I can triumph, I can unclutter my life.

The Stoning

Lord, I detest myself right now.

For I've just come from a luncheon where four of us spent most of our time criticizing a mutual friend. Her faults, her eccentricities, how extravagant and undependable she is. How she spoils her children, how vain and eager she always is to be attractive to men.

And though a lot of these things are true (Lord, they really are) I found myself wondering even as I joined in: Who are we to judge? Isn't every one of us guilty of at least some of the very same things? Was that why we attacked her with such relish? (Dear Lord, I'm so ashamed.) Because it made us feel a little bit better ourselves to brandish the defects of somebody so much "worse."

Well, I don't feel better about myself now. I keep thinking of what Jesus said to the men about to stone the adulterous woman: "Which of you is without sin?" Yet there we sat, self-righteous, stoning our sister with words.

How, Lord, can I make amends?

I long to call her up and beg her forgiveness, but that would be a terrible mistake. She would be so hurt, so much damage would be done. No, all I can do is to ask *your* forgiveness. And pray for her.

Help her, strengthen her, bless her. Don't let her ever know what we said about her, please.

And oh, Lord, put more compassion in my heart, guard my tongue. Don't let me ever again join in stoning a sister—or anyone—with words.

Order

I will trust the Lord to bring order into my life and into my house.

In his presence there can be no real chaos and confusion and dirt for he is peace and purity and order—and he is here.

He lives within these walls as he lives within my heart.

He sometimes stops me as I fret and struggle and scold, and says, "Don't be discouraged." He reminds me that we are all his untidy children, but he loves us all—even as I love these who cause me so much work.

As I move from room to room picking up other people's possessions, he reminds me how abundant is life that it strews in my family's path so many good things.

He bids me look out of the window and see the abundance of the fields, the woods, the water.

The very earth is strewn with the bright ownings and discards of its living things: sticks and branches and leaves, shells, snakeskins, nests and weeds, and feathers and flowers.

The very water carries these things on its breast. The wind blows them about.

Yet Mother Nature does not despair—no matter how many times she must do it all over.

He reminds me that back of everything, governing all, is order. Absolute order.

I will trust the Lord to bring that order into my house.

Let No Job Be Beneath Me

Thank you, God, for the wonderful gift of work. Humble work. Hard work. Brain work or back work or hand work.

I don't care much for lily-white brains and lily-white hands. I like brains that have been toughened and tried. I like backs that have been strengthened and even bent by their burdens.

I like hands that are tough, too—wrinkled from water, calloused and bruised from rocks and shovels and hammer and nails. I like hands and backs and brains that have wrestled with things, lifted and carried.

Thank you that my parents worked hard and taught their children to work hard.

Help me to remember that no job is beneath me, and with your help no job will be beyond me.

How Can Anyone Be Bored?

How can anyone possibly be bored?

So the children are grown and gone. Or you never had any children, and you've lost your life's partner. Or the job you had is over, you're retired. Whatever the reason, the days seem bleak and empty, time stretches before you like a vacuum you don't know how to fill. . . . In short, you're BORED.

But how is this possible if you are in reasonably good health, and have all your senses? How can anyone who LIVES be bored? There's so much in the world to be learned, so much in the world to do.

THE EARS alone offer so many lively paths to activity and enjoyment one couldn't take them all. Birds singing, for instance, (what a variety of little voices, what a medley of unique and vital tunes). Merely to learn about bird calls and their meaning could furnish an interest for years.

As for music! The infinite varieties of music to be listened to and understood. Blues. Jazz. Rock. Chamber music. Concertos, symphonies. Composers, performers.

When I consider the vast magical world of music and my own comparative ignorance, I am appalled. If I chose but the smallest segment of it to truly appreciate and master, there would not be enough time left in my life for its rewards. . . . While if I decide to create music myself—take up those long-abandoned violin lessons, start over from scratch on the piano, get the kinks and cobwebs out of my voice and sing in a choir.

AND WHO CAN be bored who has eyes. Art, fine art is everywhere for those not too busy to be aware—from the masterpieces in an art gallery to those in your own backyard. Whether a Raphael madonna—or a young mother bending over her baby's stroller. . . . A Dutch landscape by Vermeer —or the scene from my kitchen window. . . . An abstract by Picasso—or a puddle on a cracked sidewalk, mirroring the sky.

All the art galleries to be visited. All the dances and dramas and films to be seen. . . . And all the books—the staggering number of books, past and present, to be read!

And if you can taste, if you can smell. If you enjoy food—if you can cook. How can meals ever be a bore? Who has enough hours to try all the exciting recipes in newspapers and magazines and the constant parade of new cookbooks? Or to take all the classes in the gourmet arts? Wine tasting, cheese making, exotic fondues and curries and pates. Not to mention the enticing possibilities of organic foods.

Or if you have hands. All the arts and crafts to be explored. Sewing and quilting and macrame. The painting, the sculpture, the ceramics. The gardening, the flower arranging. A myriad of skills that can be yours. How can these hands be idle when there is beauty to be created? Or when there is so much need? Need that cries out for a few days, even a few hours of someone's time.

ABUSED OR abandoned children, the old, the helpless, the blind. Or the young who desperately need a friend. There is so much work to be done, and so many friends to be made, not only among those who need you, but those who are already helping!

How can anyone reach drearily for another cigarette or shuffle a deck of cards another pointless time? How can anyone possibly be BORED?

I'm Showing My Age

Behold, thou hast made my days as it were a span long,
and mine age is even as nothing in respect of thee.

Oh, God, dear God, I'm showing my age.

I'm not young and beautiful any more, the way my heart imagines. When I look in the mirror I could cry. For I look just what I am—a woman growing older.

And I protest it, Lord. Perhaps foolishly, I am stricken.

"Vanity, vanity, all is vanity," the Bible says. But is vanity truly such a fault? You, who made women with this instinctive hunger to hang onto personal beauty, must surely understand.

Dear God, if this be vanity, let me use it to some good purpose.

Let it inspire me to keep my body strong and well and agile, the way you made it in the beginning. May it help me to stay as attractive as possible for as long as possible—out of concern for other people as well as myself. For you, who made women, also know that when we feel attractive we're a lot easier to live with.

But oh God, whatever happens to my face and body, keep me always supple in spirit, resilient to new ideas, beautiful in the things I say and do.

If I must "show my age" let it be in some deeper dimension

of beauty that is ageless and eternal, and can only come from you.

Don't let me be so afraid of aging, God. Let me rejoice and reach out to be replenished; I know that each day I can be reborn into strength and beauty through you.

Keep Me at It

God, give me due respect for the abilities you have given me.

Don't let me sell them short. Don't let me cheapen them. Don't let me bury my talents through indecision, cowardice, or laziness.

Plant in me the necessary determination. Keep me at it.

Rouse in me the fires of dedication. Keep me at it.

Give me the energy, strength, and will power to bring your gifts to their proper fruition. Keep me at it.

When I falter or fall lift me up and set me back on my destined path. Keep me at it.

Oh, God, when the way seems dark and there is no light there, plant at least one small signal fire at the end of the long black tunnel that I may keep plodding steadily forward toward it.

When friends laugh at me, keep me at it.

When people tempt me away from it, keep me at it.

When others scorn what I have produced, let me not be discouraged. Keep me at it.

When those who have tried and failed or who have never tried at all, those who are envious or indolent, when such people would hurt me by spiteful words or acts, let me not be bothered. Return me to my task. Keep me at it.

Let nothing really matter but these precious gifts you have entrusted to me. For their sake let me be willing and proud to make the sacrifice. Keep me at it.

The Missing Ingredient

Lord, I have all the ingredients for happiness in my life. A lovely home, a wonderful husband. Children, friends, health. Why then is there such a sense of vacancy in me? Why this glum feeling of futility, even sometimes despair?

It's as if I keep expecting something glorious to happen that part of me is afraid is never *going* to happen. Some added flavor that's lacking, some challenge. Snug and safe and lucky (oh, so lucky) I press my disconsolate nose against the shining picture windows of my nest.

I want a parade to come by instead of just seeing kids climbing off a school bus. I want a limousine full of mysterious and exciting people to sweep up to the curb instead of a fuel-oil truck. I want the world to cry, "Come out, come out, you brilliant, beautiful thing! Why are you wasting yourself there?"

I want some glamor, some drama, some attention. I want to do something *important*.

I know, Lord—yes, yes, I know that making a home, raising a family *are* important. And that when the house is cold, better a fuel-oil man than a diplomat. So give me a sensible scale of values, give me patience.

But don't make me too sensible either. Don't give me too much patience. Maybe this is a "divine discontent" to keep me from getting sluggish, complacent. Maybe this hunger for some missing ingredient in my life is simply a way of telling me: "If you want something exciting to happen, you've got to *make* it happen." . . . Join a theater group or start one. Take a class or teach one. Find a job or create one. Sing, paint, write, dance. Help others who don't have the things I'm so blessed with and don't always appreciate.

Maybe you *meant* women like me to grow restless, in order to give our full measure to a world that has been so good to us.

Cut Back the Vines

"Go cut back the grapes," I tell my son. "They're too thick, they've practically taken over the garage."

Naturally he has urgent business elsewhere; but after the usual argument he grabs the pruning shears and dashes outdoors. I hear him whacking away.

I look out later, and am aghast. The garage walls are naked. He has severed the lush growth clear back to the ground. "You've ruined them!" I accuse. "We'll never have grapes there again."

Wrong. The grapes came back the following year with an abundance never known before; great purple clusters, fat and sweet, so heavy they bowed the trellis. It was just as Jesus said: "Every branch in me that beareth not fruit he taketh away: and every branch that beareth fruit, he purgeth it, that it may bring forth more fruit" (John 15:2).

I thought of the ruthless slashing. The seeming waste. My scolding protests and my son's innocent bewilderment—he'd thought it was what I wanted. Our misunderstanding. The great fire we had to have even to dispose of the old branches . . . And now this! The newer, stronger, invigorated vines. The harvest so plentiful we carried basketsful to the neighbors.

"He purgeth it. . . ." Pain and problems, the conflicts and disappointments, the defeats, the tragedies to which we all are subject—are they not purgings? I look back on my life sometimes in amazement before the memories of those terrible cuttings. Those times of trial by fire, it seemed . . . Intolerable,

intolerable. Rescue me, spare me! . . . Yet now I realize they were essential to my growth. How much hostility had to go in the process, how much self-pity, how much pride. A tangle of choking, life-impeding habits threatening to deny all that God meant me to be. I, too, had to be cut back, laid low.

And somehow, in the midst of it, I realized I could not go it alone, Lord. It was too much. I could not handle the weight of it, the people, the problems, the family, my job as a wife and mother, my fate as a woman in this demanding world, without support beyond my own.

Those words in John—all of them—must have been written for me: "Abide in me, and I in you. As the branch cannot bear fruit of itself, except it abide in the vine; no more can ye, except ye abide in me.

"I am the vine, ye are the branches: He that abideth in me, and I in him, the same bringeth forth much fruit: for without me ye can do nothing" (John 15:4-5).

It was like that. I saw that without you I could do nothing. You are the vine, not me. Weak and faulty as I was, I'd been trying to be the vine, holding up all the branches. I was just a branch and I had to be pruned, I had to be stripped if my roots were to be strengthened. Then only then could I bring forth much fruit!

For Every Cross I've Carried

Thank you, God, for every cross I have ever had to carry. For every burden I have ever had to bear. For every honest tear I have ever shed.

Thank you for my troubles—they give me courage.

Thank you for my afflictions—they teach me compassion.

Thank you for my disappointments—through them I learn humility and am inspired to try harder again.

Thank you that in fashioning this world you didn't see fit to spare us from the evil you knew would be there. Thank you for not keeping us like dumb animals in a corral. That, instead, you freed us, gave us the dignity of making our own decisions, even if it also meant we must stumble and fall and suffer in order to rise again.

Thank you that in every aspect of our lives you are always near us. Loving, protecting, helping. Hearing our prayers and giving us the strength to endure what we must for our own souls' growth.

I know you, Lord, in times of peace and plenty. But when life is easy it's too easy to forget you; I don't need you quite so much. When life is tough, however, when I see nothing about me but trouble and torment, then I must find you, I must have you! I go crying to you through the darkness, knowing that though the whole world forsake me you will not turn away.

My very suffering brings you near.

Self-pity

Lord, all night I lay awake consorting with self-pity.

Its idiot voice would not let me sleep. It entertained me with its chant of woes.

It pursued me into the pillow when I tried to bury my head. When I turned to the right it was there, insidiously smiling; when I turned to the left it perched upon my bed.

I thrust it aside but it would not leave me; it would not let me go. And though I finally slept, when I awoke this morning, it trailed me into the kitchen triumphant.

It was not satisfied that it had robbed me of rest; it wanted to sit beside me at breakfast, to tag me about all day. It pursues, it clutches at me still.

God, I am asking you to purge me of this awful companion now. I offer it up to you to do with what you will.

Take self-pity away. Banish it. Heal me of its scars.

Please put self-respect, and a vital glowing sense of the many marvels and blessings of my life in its place.

Just for Today

Oh, God, give me grace for this day.

Not for a lifetime, nor for next week, nor for tomorrow, just for this day.

Direct my thoughts and bless them.

Direct my work and bless it.

Direct the things I say, and give them blessing too.

Direct and bless everything that I think and speak and do. So that for this one day, just this one day, I have the gift of grace that comes from your presence.

Oh, God, for this day, just this one day, let me live generously, kindly, in a state of grace and goodness that denies my many imperfections and makes me more like you.

To Witness Suffering

Oh, God, this suffering . . . to be helpless witness to another person's suffering.

It seems that my own I could bear more easily. At least I could cry out lustily, bloodily. I could wrestle it, fight it, put up a mighty battle.

But this—to be whole and strong, every sense vivid and vulnerable, and be forced to attend a love one's agony. To hear the cries and witness the struggle yet be powerless to put an end to it.

Or to have to be brave because the sufferer is so brave. To be cheerful when the heart is breaking. To live within sight and sound and touch of the endless suffering, essential to the victim's very existence.

I cry out against this sometimes, Lord. Even as I beg deliverance for the sufferer, or that some of these torments be put upon me instead. Why do you allow it? What earthly good is such suffering? And why have I been cast in this role?

Then I realize that you are not the author of suffering, but that you alone can take our suffering and turn it to some good purpose. What that purpose is I don't know, only that it *is*.

Surely for that reason you made me unusually strong, resilient, enduring. Able to comfort if only by not breaking down. Able to share some modicum of that strength.

Lord, when I think I can endure this no longer, let me remember those who did not flee the scene of the cross.

Help me to keep my vigil with suffering as courageously as they kept theirs.

The Box in the Attic

This box of college keepsakes, God. I don't know whether to laugh or cry, going through them. I don't know whether to wrap them up tenderly again or pitch them out.

The cups and medals so tarnished, the photographs of glory, hopelessly dated, poor things. And these dry, faded flowers . . . how could I ever have thought their colors would last? They're ghost flowers now. This whole box is filled with nothing but ghost memories, ghost promises . . .

The speaking contests won. The plays when everybody said I had so much talent, ought to go to New York, become a star. Here are some of the old programs, here is the dusty velvet costume I wore as Desdemona. I hold it up forlornly, half amused, half guilty—I couldn't even get into it any more!

"Promises, promises," as the saying goes. Promises unfulfilled. And I wonder—have I failed life, Lord? Or has life failed me?

Or has there been any failure at all?

How do I know I'd ever have gotten to Broadway if I'd tried? Or become a star? Or been any happier if I had? And isn't the role I'm playing now just as important as any I'd have there? (The work is steadier, that's sure, and the rewards, though less spectacular, are surely a lot more lasting.)

So I wonder, trying to sort out this box in the attic, what should I be feeling—regret, or relief? Should I weep for my wasted talents, or should I be thankful that I've avoided the grim old-fashioned work and heartbreak it takes to succeed on the stage? (Not that there isn't plenty of that in being a wife and mother! And I *am* a star . . . well, anyway a co-star of this family.)

Yet something nags at me yet, Lord. A restlessness I can't rationalize away. These tarnished, tattered, faintly ludicrous souvenirs—they are a kind of mute accusing testimony. I did have talent once. And talent is precious, talent means responsibility. Like that story in the Bible, when you give somebody talent you don't expect it to be buried.

Have I buried my talent, Lord, or only put it away for safekeeping? Surely there are places where I can use my talent still. And for better purposes now than just to satisfy my own ambition. Surely, without neglecting anybody, I can find outlets right here—little theater, coaching children, helping out with plays for charity.

I can't repolish the loving cups, let out the costumes, refurbish these souvenirs. But I can polish up my own gifts, let out my own horizons, reactivate *me!* Instead of mooning over past triumphs, I can get going on tomorrow's.

Thank you, Lord, for leading me to this box of keepsakes in the attic.

I'm Tired of Being Strong

Forgive me, Lord, but I'm tired of being some of the things I've tried so hard to be.

I'm tired of being so capable, so efficient. I'm tired of the compliment, "If you want to get something done ask a busy person." (Guess who?)

I'm tired of being considered so patient and understanding that people dump their troubles (and their kids) on me.

I'm tired of being so cheerful. I want to be free to be cross and complain and not get a "buck up, old girl," routine. I'm tired of being my husband's faithful partner and helpmate instead of his playmate.

I'm tired of being considered so independent, so strong.

Sometimes, at least sometimes, Lord, I want to be weak and helpless, able to lean on somebody, able to cry and be comforted.

Lord, I guess there are just times when I want to be a little girl again, running to climb on my mother's lap.

The Suffering Few of Us Escape

You know what a coward I am about suffering, God. My own or other people's.

I would never have made a martyr; once they started to beat me or drag me to the lions I'm afraid I'd have recanted. If I were imprisoned and they tortured me for secrets, I don't think I could stand it—I'd tell!

And I am sickened before the spectacle of suffering, any physical suffering, of man or animal. (How can anyone be entertained by brutal acts? How can anyone cheer at the sight of any creature bruised, bleeding, struggling desperately to escape?)

It's hard for me even to READ about suffering. If I am helpless to stop it, it seems witless to punish my own flesh and soul by drinking in the dread details. . . .

No, no, I must flee from physical suffering.

Yet there is another kind of suffering few of us can flee. And that we cannot stop by a mere act of will: not by averting our eyes, running away, slamming the door.

The agony of love in all its variations.

Man and woman love. The many aspects of love between male and female . . . Anxiety about the one so close to us . . . Long separations . . . Conflicts, quarrels, doubts . . . Husband and wife who've forgotten how to talk to each other . . . Indifference . . . The bitter wounds of unfaithfulness . . . To be denied the person most deeply loved . . . The awful unfulfilled hungers of body and soul . . .

These our private crucifixions.

And children: O God, dear God, the multiple crucifixions we undergo for our children. Nailed to the cross again and again for their shortcomings. Or only waiting at the cross sometimes (which can be worse) forced to witness their suffering.

So I am no stranger to suffering. And I can't honestly call myself a coward before these emotional assaults. In some ways I feel brave before them. I have faced them before, most of them, and will face them again and survive. You give me the strength, you give me the courage.

You make me realize that anyone who drinks from the sweet cup of love must also swallow the gall. But love is worth it . . . ah, but it's worth it! And if you are truly love, as Jesus taught, then the price we pay for love has even more value.

In suffering for love of others we are also suffering for love of you. This suffering I welcome, Lord.

Let Me Say "Yes" to New Experiences

Lord, don't let me be afraid to say "Yes" to new experiences. New places to go, new people to meet, new things to learn. Don't let me be a coward about trying things—new friends or new foods, new books or new music, new inventions, new ideas.

Sure, it's safer and a lot less trouble just to chug along in the same old rut. But that way lies age and stagnation. The young are so willing to *try* things. And while you didn't design us to stay young forever, if I'd created a world so gloriously full of creatures, places and adventures, I'd be sad to see my children cowering in corners, refusing to discover its surprises—at least until they had to.

Lord, thank you for helping me overcome sheer laziness and dread:

Dread of travel. Half-eager to go, half-miserable before the complexities and problems any trip presents. How much easier not to have to shop, pack, cope with tickets and arrangements. Just to stay home where things are familiar. Yet how grateful I am for having made the effort. My life's store of friendships, knowledge and memories is enriched because of every trip I've taken.

Dread of sports, physical challenge. Learning to swim and dive and skate, learning to ski and ride and play tennis. The voices that whimper and warn, especially as we get older: "The water's cold," or "You might get hurt," or "Stay here where it's warm and cozy. Who *needs* this?" Lord, don't let me give up the things I already can do, or give in to the voices that would stop me from at least attempting new ones. The back porch may be more secure, but the fun is in jumping the fences . . .

Dread of meeting new people. Even the friends now so dear to me were once sometimes frightening strangers. Yet you led me to them, Lord, often against my own resistance. And my life would be empty without them.

God, don't ever take away my courage to try things.

Forgiving Means Forgetting

I don't find it too hard to forgive, Lord—what's hard is to forget.

When someone is truly sorry I think, "Yes, yes, I forgive you." Just to have the estrangement over, to be relieved of the awful pain of being parted even mentally from someone I love. In sheer self-protection I think I "forgive."

But the memory remains. Deep, buried deep inside me, the deed or the word still lives. And it rises sometimes to taunt me, to wreck the peace I've achieved.

Why, Lord? Why do these memories linger?

Is it because I've forgiven for the wrong reasons? Selfish reasons. Not genuine compassion and love and charity for the other person and his human frailties, but for myself. Me—me—me. Because I can't stand to be so hurt.

Help me to change this, Lord. Make me strong enough to forgive people out of love rather than a mere frantic desire to ease my own wounds. Forgive so wholly, fully, in such a flood there is no room for nagging memories.

Thank you for teaching me to forgive this way. True forgiving means forgetting.

God Says, "Get Up!"

Again and again God says, "Get up!"

Sometimes he speaks through people, and it seems a harsh, unfeeling physical command. . . . I am ill. Pain-wracked. Anyone can see I'm in no condition to leave my bed. Yet the doctor and the nurses enter, and to my astonishment say, "Let's get you up awhile today. You must get up."

Sometimes it is but the voice of the stern but loving command of the God without and within. . . . I am prostrate with grief, my life is in shambles, there is nothing left for me now but the terrible comfort of my tears. . . . Dimly, beyond drawn shades, I realize the world is going on heartlessly about its business. People pass by, some of them even laughing, outside on the street. . . . The telephone rings. There is a knocking at my door.

I stuff my ears, try to burrow deeper into my awful loss. Then the voice comes strong and clear: "Get up."

"I can't, I can't. . . . O, God I can't."

It comes again. This time more imperative than the telephone or the doorbell or the awareness of duties to people who need me. "Get up!"

Startled, I stagger to my feet. . . . Grope protestingly for some means of support—and find it. A chair to lean on, or unexpectedly the arm of a friend . . . But in a few minutes I realize I won't need them, for there is another support beside me. God has provided the brace. He would not call me back to action otherwise. He will sustain me.

It is so easy to "quench my thirst with tears and so learn to love my sorrows," as the Paulist priest James Carroll wrote. So easy, and often so tempting, to fall in love with our own misfortunes. For that way lies sympathy (if sometimes only self-sympathy) and possible escape. . . .

We're tired, fed up with this rat race, this drudgery; we don't want to work. . . . "Get up. Do it!"

We are ill and nurturing our own illness. . . . "Get up. Get well."

We are stricken with sorrow or shame; our troubles overpower us, we long only to sink into the slough of our despondency behind locked doors. . . . The command rings loud and clear: "You cannot bury yourself any longer. Get up! Get on with living."

Again and again Jesus said those words. To people lying in sickbeds or even on deathbeds: "Arise! Get up." And they did, and were well and lived again. He is saying them still to anyone who will listen: "Don't give in to your pain and problems. Don't nourish your grief. Get up."

Thank you, Lord, for never failing to say them to me.

Life is too short and too sweet to squander in the darkness, crying. Thank God, thank God you always get me up and back into action. This, as nothing else could, proves how much you care for me.

Don't Let Me Stop Growing

Don't let me ever stop growing, God. Mentally growing.

This mind you have given me (any mind!) has such marvelous potential. Why should I hobble it to a house, shackle it to a kitchen sick, cuddle down with it behind a coffee clache?

It's tempting, Lord, and all too easy to give up, make excuses, do the most comfortable thing. To settle for small talk, small interests, small horizons. I've seen this happen to so many women, some of my brightest friends. No wonder they're bored, God. Restless and bored. And boring.

Don't let this happen to me. Let me learn at least one new thing about something important every day. (Well, at least every other day.) Let no day pass without reading. Keep my mind always open, lively, reaching out for new interests, new knowledge.

Don't let me stop mentally growing.

Keep me always growing, God. Emotionally growing.

Help me outgrow my tears, my sometimes childish tantrums. The periods of self-pity when I tell myself nobody loves me, like I used to as a little girl. Please rescue me whenever I revert; steer me firmly forward into the calm waters of mature behavior. Let me feel the thrill of self-command, the dignity of self-control.

I want to keep emotionally growing.

Help me to keep growing, God, in relation to others.
So many people need me, depend on me, look to me for

help, for answers. And I so often feel inadequate, unequal to their demands. Sometimes I even feel impatient and resentful, not wanting to be bothered. (Why should they drain my time and energy?) Forgive me for this feeling, Lord, and fortify my reserves.

Broaden my understanding. Deepen my compassion. Give me more wisdom and joy in sharing when I can.

As a wife, mother or friend, help me to keep growing.

Don't let me ever stop growing, God. Spiritually growing. Drawing ever closer to you, the source of it all: The universe. The world and the life upon it. The people . . . the person . . . myself.

I want to know you better, tune in more truly with the harmonies of all your creation, including the life that is my own.

Thank you for this person that you made in your image, Lord. Don't let me ever stop growing.

Possessions

Help me not to put too much stock in possessions, Lord. Mere possessions.

I want things, sure I want things. Life seems to be a continual round of wanting things, from the first toys we fight over as children, on through our thrilled counting of the wedding presents . . . Not primarily love and friends and pride in what we can do, but *things*.

Sometimes I'm ashamed of how much I want things. For my husband and the house and the children. Yes, and for myself. And this hunger is enhanced every time I turn on the TV or walk through a shopping mall. My senses are tormented by the dazzling world of *things*.

Lord, cool these fires of wanting. Help me to realize how futile is this passion for possession. Because—and this is what strips my values to the bone—one of my best friends died today in the very midst of her possessions.

The beautiful home she and her husband worked so hard to achieve, finally finished; furnished the way she wanted it, with the best of everything . . . The oriental rugs she was so proud of. The formal French sofas. The paintings. The china and glass and handsome silver service . . . She has been snatched away, while silently, almost cruelly, they remain.

Lord, I grieve for my friend. My heart hurts that she had so little time to enjoy her things. Things she had earned and that meant so much to her. But let me learn something from this loss:

That possessions are meant to enhance life, not to become the main focus of living. That we come into the world with nothing, we leave with nothing.

Help me not to put too much stock in mere possessions.

I Must Depend on Myself

Thank you, Lord, that there are so many people I can depend on for so many things. My husband and children. My neighbors and friends. The people with whom I work. I know I can count on any one of them—most of the time, at least—to do things for me, often without being asked. Just as they know they can count on me to help them.

But there is another person I must learn to depend on even more, Lord: *Myself*. You gave each of us areas of life where we *can't* lean on anybody else.

Nobody else can do our exercises, stick to our diets, study our courses, take our exams. Nobody else can read or write our books, sing our solos, dream our dreams, execute our plans. Nobody else can get our lives organized, productive and moving in the direction of our goals.

In short, Lord, no other person can keep my promises—to others or to me. For that, all that, I've got to depend on myself.

Help me to remember this. God, give me belief in myself and the will power to act on that belief. Thank you for gradually guiding me into habits that fortify that faith, so that at the end of each day I can realize: "I didn't let me down. I did what I promised myself!"

And even when I undertake too much, set my sights too high, project goals a little beyond my reach, help me not to get discouraged. Rather, to realize that delay doesn't mean defeat. Despite a hundred detours, I will keep driving in the right direction.

I will not quit. I will keep my commitments.

Thank you for giving me a clear, honest awareness of this, God, and the courage to live by that truth. Make me always able to depend on myself.

An American Woman's Prayer

Thank you, God. First and foremost that I'm a woman. What's more, an American woman—that luckiest of all possible beings. For nowhere else in the whole wide world could I be so respected, so cherished, so privileged (some people call it downright spoiled) and yet so free.

Thank you that I can vote or run for office (and win too). That I can marry or not, have children or not, work or not, and it's nobody's business but my own; there's nobody really to stop me but me.

Thank you that, although discrimination dies hard (men have run your world so long, God, and forgive me but you made men proud and slow to change), no doors are really closed to me. I can be a doctor—surgeon, dentist, vet. I can be a lawyer, I can be a judge. I can dance, swim, act—be an artist, drive a truck, umpire a baseball game. I can work in forests or harvest fields as well as offices if it suits me.

But, dear Lord, how I thank you that my government doesn't *make* me do any of these things. I can stay home and be a wife and mother if I please. I can be my own boss as I cook and sew and chase the kids and clean. (And while I'm at it, thank you for the marvelous conveniences that make keeping house in America easier than anyplace else on earth.)

Thank you, God, for the prosperity and plenty of this incredible country. The abundance of our resources—coal and oil and water and grain, and human energy and skill. For you know how hard we've worked to get where we are. Unlike the skeptical hireling of the parable, we didn't just bury the gifts you gave us, but plowed and sowed and sweat and made them bear fruit. And then, with arms and hearts overflowing, we rushed to the whole world's aid.

Thank you that we inherited not only our forefathers' and mothers' achievements but their generosity, their willingness to share. That never in all our history have we turned our back on another nation in need.

Thank you, God, that my children were born in this remarkable land. *Born free.* Daughters as well as sons, just as free as I am to do with their lives what they will.

Oh, help us truly to value that freedom, God, and guard it well. Don't let us take it for granted. Don't let us become weak, soft, vulnerable. So afraid of being considered old-fashioned, so eager to be sophisticated, modern, that we play into the hands of those who would take it away.

Don't let us discount it, downgrade it. And dear God, make us just as quick to praise our country's virtues and triumphs and blessings as we are to criticize. For who can do his best—man, woman, child or nation—if no credit is ever forthcoming? No appreciation—only blame?

Help us to stop criticizing *ourselves* so much, God. Restrain our own breast beating. Help us to remember that no nation since the beginning of time has ever had even half the freedom and advantages we enjoy.

Light in us fervent new fires of patriotism, Lord.

Patriotism. A word of passionate honor in almost every country except the one that deserves it so much! Make us proud to be American patriots once again. Willing to shout our heritage from the housetops. Let us thrill once more to the sight of our star-spangled banner. May it fly from every flagpole, be honored in every schoolroom. Let us and our children pledge our allegiance to it wherever Americans gather, and sing the words of its anthem with love and thanksgiving.

Oh, Lord, dear Lord, remind us: We are so *lucky* to be Americans. And I'm so lucky to be an American woman.

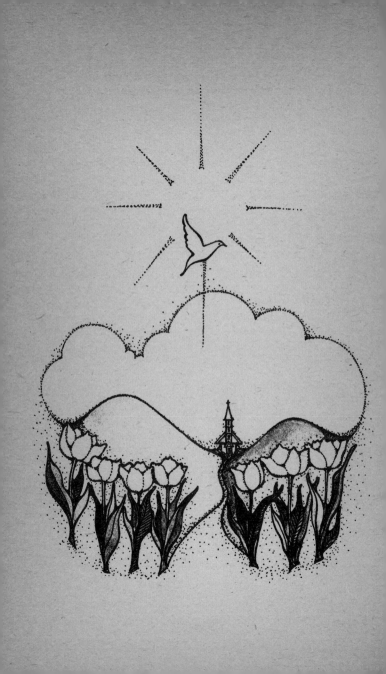

God
Love

To Love, to Labor

I am trying to find God.

Secretly, desperately, so many busy people are trying to find God. But we can't, we think we can't because we *are* so busy. Going to church to worship God takes time (precious time when we need to rest from all our busyness); meetings to talk about God take time. Prayers and meditation take time. . . . Peace, leisure, quiet . . . let me alone, give me a vacation away from my job and the family, let me walk along the seashore, climb a mountain, camp in the solitude of a forest. There I'll find God waiting and I can relax and say, "At last. I've been dying to meet you, have you over, come in!"

But the people of life keep clambering all over us, the business of life won't let us escape. Or if solitude, long postponed, is somehow achieved, are we comfortable with this stranger, God, are we sure he's even there?

No, no, if I am to know him, truly know him, neither of us can wait. What then? Take God along to work? *That* rat race? Absurd. Work is the result of God's enemy. Weren't Adam and Eve happy playing in the Garden (and walking and talking with God) until Satan ruined everything? They were driven out for their folly, and their punishment was to labor: "In the sweat of thy face shalt thou eat bread, till thou return unto the ground . . ." (Gen. 3:19).

So labor became a fact of life. The most important fact, actually, for most of us must work to survive. And work can indeed be punishment: work you detest, work that seems to be leading nowhere. But punishment is generally meant not to damage but to strengthen us. And that long-ago Lord of our beginnings knew it: No more handouts, no more childlike idling. . . . Toil, sweat, achieve, *grow*. . . . I made you, now make something of yourselves.

Back of that eviction curse lurked a blessing. The Creator was doing us all a favor, he was enriching the whole human race.

How glorious that you drove man from the Garden, God. How wise of you, how glorious! You saw that they would not have been complete in the Garden, undeveloped as children, playing children's games. You foresaw that they wouldn't have been happy, for there is no real joy in idleness, no challenge, no satisfaction.

Until they were forced to labor, procreate and labor, they could never become true people. Living, breathing, striving people, able to taste fruits far more sweet than that first forbidden apple: the fruits of their labor.

You gave them—and us—the gift of sweat, the salty baptism of our own toil. You gave us the sweetness of rest after a hard day's work. You gave us the satisfaction of accomplishment, the joy of a job well done. And you gave us goals, the dream of greater achievements to come.

And you foresaw that only in labor can there be love, true love. Man for woman, woman for man, and both of them for their children.

For we labor for those we love. And love sweetens that labor and the labor cements that love.

I can't imagine a world without work. Surely it would be an empty, meaningless world. A world without God in it.

The Trees

We seek you in people, God. We try to find you in churches; we hunt you diligently in books. And all the while your reality is everywhere around us, simply awaiting recognition. Your messages are written in the landscape if we'll only look.

Brother Lawrence, the seventeenth-century monk who left such a beautiful legacy in his *Practice of the Presence of God*, was converted by the mere sight on a midwinter day "of a dry and leafless tree standing gaunt against the snow; it stirred deep thoughts within him of the change the coming spring would bring. From that moment on he grew and waxed strong in the knowledge and love and favor of God."

Years ago in suburban Philadelphia . . . my tree. A great oak whose branches scraped the attic window where I had fixed up a cubby with books and papers. My cozy high retreat. There I could sometimes flee when the storms of life seemed almost too much to bear. . . . Lie across the couch "having a good bawl," as my mother used to say. Grappling with a woman's private agonies . . . Mine, rejection slips piled as high as the dishes in the sink . . . The daily tearing asunder as children, desperately loved, wove maddeningly in and out of my study with their tears and little treasures and demands . . . A husband I was lucky to see once or twice a week . . . And now this—after three years of editorial encouragement and personal sacrifice, the return of the novel that would (I thought) solve everything.

Rain pouring down to match my tears . . . The plaintive screech and scratch across the glass, then tap-tap-tap as if something was begging to come in . . . Go fling up the window, break off the offending branch. Yet there with the coldness on my face, something held me. Some majesty of motion—this greater thing than I swaying and keening and uttering its own cries into the wind. Its permanence spoke to me, its great age. It had lived long before me and would go on living, no doubt, long after I was gone. Blind, deaf, unfeeling, how could it know anything about me? And yet it spoke to me, comforted me in a way I could not articulate.

Later, when it was dark, I remember going down and putting on a son's old hooded mackinaw and creeping out in the rain to embrace that tree. Self-dramatics? Maybe. But I wanted to put my arms around its great girth, feel its bark against my cheeks. It had something to give me no human being could. Just what, I didn't know. Only that it stirred in me some deep sense of protection and faith. God, my long-neglected God, had created that tree.

If he could do that, he could do anything! He could look after me.

These moments of awareness, Lord. These powerful moments of conviction. Why can't we hang on to them? Why do we let them slip away?

Yet they are not in vain. Looking back, we remember them with a kind of puzzled wonder. Looking forward, even during the times when we feel hopelessly lost and groping, something tells us they will come again.

And if we will listen, truly look and listen, there is no stopping them. They will happen over and over.

They will happen now!

God has so much to say to us through the trees. Lie on your back and read his eloquent sermons in the trees. . . .

A chill but sun-gilded February day. I stretch out on a wooden bench in the yard and gaze up at the sky. And all about me rise the trees, naked, stripped, revealed. They are like nude dancers stretching . . . stretching . . . glorying in their lovely bones. How incredibly tall they are and how straight they grow. The trunks in almost every cluster soar unswerving toward the sky, as if intent upon their goal. Yet their branches reach out . . . out . . . a little uplifted as if in adoration or rejoicing. They are in an attitude of dancing or of prayer. And I see that they are open, so very open, as if to give and to receive.

What blessings pour down upon those grateful arms. Sun and wind and snow and rain and lightening wings. They are merry with squirrels; and at night they wear stars in their fingers.

They are open for giving as well. They are lively with birds, they hold their nests for safekeeping. Soon these outstretched arms will be bursting with buds and flowers and leaves. They will spread their fragrance and their shade. Nuts will rain down from these generous arms, fruit will clot their branches and be claimed by other arms, upreaching. Or the fruit will fall by its very abundance, too much for the boughs, so richly receiving and giving, to contain.

And it is all a matter of the sturdy central trunk, undiverted on its skyward journey, yet accompanied, always accompanied by these happy, open, spreading arms. . . .

The design—the perfect design for tree or man. To be strong in central purpose, heading toward the destination meant for us, but open, always open both to give and to receive.

Why Am I Working Here?

This work you have given me, God. This job I seem doomed, at least right now, to do.

Why do I hate it sometimes, struggle so against its demands? Why do I so often drag myself to the appointed place and anticipate the day I must spend there as a form of penalty?

Why does it sometimes seem unworthy of me and the abilities you have given me? . . . Is this true, Lord? *Is* it unworthy, or am I unworthy of it?"

Help me sort out these confusions, God. To recognize, in a very practical, earthy sense, why I am performing this particular service during this particular time of my life upon the earth, and if it is really what you want me to do.

For I must find you in my work. Work is a part of life. You are a part of life—the very source of these hands, these feet, this brain.

Whether I am scrubbing a floor, pounding a typewriter, fixing a car, digging a mine, operating a machine . . . whether I am coping with personnel problems or an unruly classroom . . . I am earning my keep upon this planet, I am paying my way in human coin. And quietly, inflexibly back of the whole design, you are.

Is this seemingly empty, disagreeable labor a time of humbling? To show me I am of the selfsame stuff as my brothers and sisters—no worse, no better?

I, too, can lift and carry, argue, cope, hurt, get dirty, do things I dislike or things I consider beneath my so-called dignity.

Am I being tried for self-denial? Self-control? Am I being tested for appreciation? To be thankful that I have the means to earn my daily bread, and the ability to see its small but sure rewards (the shining floor . . . the ledgers that balance . . . the children progressing . . . the nuggets of coal).

Or is this a time of training, Lord? Of preparation for more vital challenges ahead? Of learning—every day, hour by hour, even though I can't see it—the skills and qualities I'm going to need?

This I know, Lord. This much I know and must remember: Nothing is wasted. Nothing is fruitless—no work that you give us to do. If it is of you—decent work, honorable work, work that helps mankind in any way instead of harming it—then that work is effective.

It affects my life's development, body and soul. And it affects everyone around me. My family; the people who work beside me. And all the younger lives it touches, they are marked by my work, too.

Help me to realize this fact, to accept it and even glory in it. For now, for now, for as long as you really want to use me in this manner . . . But let me always be open to change. Alert for the voice that calls, "Come! You're ready for something else." Hopefully, something better. But at least the next step on the ladder of my life.

Until that time comes, I am resolved to return to my job rejoicing.

Giving more to it.
Getting more out of it.
Learning more from it.
And thanking you.

Sight on a Moonlit Road

The leaves are still frail and new, a tremulous green dusting upon these tall old trees. And just below them the dogwoods are a delicate white mist of bloom. Only a red suggestion of buds a few days ago, now the flat, faintly cupped petals are upheld, like some display of precious china in a jeweler's window.

The moon enhances their translucent purity. The very roadway, dark by day, is white with its flooding.

The black and white dog bounding along ahead has a luminous quality. And the cat, which has slipped out and pats silently behind, is also shining. White face and paws echo the Dalmatian's spotted body in tinier dots that weave through the shadows. Like little floating stars or petals in the fragrant chirping night.

A utility pole beside the road is illuminated too, its black spear and crossbar moon-rimmed. Turning, I see its startling shadow lying across the moon-white road.

A cross! A leaning cross, moon-etched. Tender, graceful, and not really sad. Only poignant. A poignant reminder of suffering. The Lord's suffering and triumph. All human suffering and triumph.

A moving sight on a moonlit roadway.

A Potato

I am peeling a potato.

What a homely thing it is, this lumpy ellipse in my hand. Brown, earth-brown, with the dust of the earth clinging to it. Yet as my knife strips away its humble skin, how moistly pure and white it is inside. Solid yet succulent, rich with the nourishment drawn from the darkness in which it lay.

Contrasts—all these contrasts. The light and the dark, the buried and the risen. The continuing miracle ready to spring from the ordinary things of everyday . . . How amazing this is. What secret treasures the silent soil holds. And how little we have to know and be to tap them . . . A potato! This potato.

If I were to save even a chunk of it, a piece with an eye in it, and bury it, it would become another plant bursting forth with leaves and flowers to inform me when it was ready, that it had flung about it hidden nuggets to be dug. Offering me more potatoes than I would need for a week . . . Such abundance!

And such magic. That this mealy whiteness soon to feed my family emerged from the mute black stuff beneath my feet. Dirt, plain dirt. Dirt that we get on our shoes and are forever trying to drive out of our houses. Low, common, spurned, yet vital to the whole life plan, and during this existence, at least, never to be escaped. It upholds me every step I take. And though I may fly from it by plane and flee from it by boat, it is the substance to which I must always return. I am earthbound. Chains of gravity hold me to the earth, and the even more powerful chain of life itself. Its grains and its grasses feed me, and so do its trees with their nuts and fruit. Except for fish, every creature that nourishes me likewise must draw its own nourishment from the earth. While deep in its body it carries fuels to warm me, minerals and elements to build and serve me in a thousand ways.

Scientists in their laboratories might be able to duplicate synthetically all its elements. They can and have made artificial substances in which things will grow. Yet what of the organisms that exist in that soil, the microbes, the bacteria, the bugs and worms? Even a teaspoon of soil. A thimbleful, a pinch. In *The Secret Life of Plants* the authors tell how the famous oceanographer William Beebe occupied himself during a long sea journey by analyzing a small bag of earth mold. "And found in it over five hundred separate specimens of life. He believed that more than twice that many remained to be identified."

Soil squirms and breathes and lives, it draws life into itself and gives life back.

And so—this potato . . . Brown with the same earth from which human beings came, and the earth to which we must return.

I think of Genesis. First two chapters. Turn the fire low and read them. . . . The simplicity. The absolute directness and purity of the story of creation. God so busy about his monumental task:

And the earth was without form, and void; and darkness was upon the face of the deep.

Try to imagine. I can't. But God (or something) imposed order. Brought light, divided night from day and sea from land.

And let the dry land appear: and it was so.

And God called the dry land Earth; and the gathering together of the waters called he Seas: and God saw that it was good.

And God said, Let the earth bring forth grass, the herb yielding seed, and the fruit tree yielding fruit after his kind, whose seed is in itself, upon the earth: and it was so.

And the earth brought forth grass, and herb yielding seed after his kind, and the tree yielding fruit, whose seed was in itself, after his kind: and God saw that it was good.

There is something very tender and moving about that. Someone, or something, wanted things to be so right for us. Everything in readiness and plenty of it—so much, so much. And when every last thing had been done, he took a bit of dust from the ground:

and breathed into his nostrils the breath of life; and man became a living soul.

I once dismissed all this as a pretty myth. But only out of my own ignorance and futility, my helplessness to understand. I tried to replace it with formulas and theory (I didn't understand those either, but I thought they sounded more intelligent). Now I see that it is really more intelligent to acknowledge the marvel as simply beyond understanding. But that someone or something indeed "saw that it was good." Not chaos but order. Not poisonous but life-sustaining. And the most remarkable creation of all emerged from the mystery: man with his mind and his choices and his indestructible soul.

There is something tender and moving, too—and to me almost funny—that this Creator chose the dirt for our source. Why not a drop of water or the petal of a flower? Nothing so delicate or aesthetic—no, a bit of the rich yet humble dust! . . . So I am akin to this potato and everything that grows. For this dust, this very dust that I am rinsing away right now, provides all the building stuff of my body. And when that body is no more use, it will return to the ground.

Strange.

Allegorical language has a way of distilling and preserving deep instinctive truths. We speak of the good earth, Mother Earth. And we call God our Father. The one who created this earth and richly seeded her to produce this whole family I belong to—the family of man. We are indeed children of the earth, as we are children of our earthly parents. And all this makes us children of God.

The Garden

This is my garden, God, this is my garden, my own small precious portion of the earth that you have made.

I will dig and hoe and tend it, I will grub in the soil that is cool and moist and scented with spring.

I will find you in that soil as I crumble its clods or press these small seeds deep into its dark flesh.

What a joyful thing, the feel of your silent soil. It clings to my fingers, it is hard and certain beneath my knees.

It receives my little offerings—these tiny plants, these slips and cuttings, these infinitesimal seedlings, with a kind of blind, uncommenting magnificence. I am a trifle awed before it, I am filled with an amused humility.

How insignificant I am that I should be entrusted with this miracle to come. No, no, the earth will surely reject my anxious efforts, my foolish hopes. Yet I know a happy patience too. Wait—only wait upon the Lord, as the Bible says.

And sure enough. The silent, teeming forces of creation set to work, and soon the miracle has come! Onions and lettuce for the table. Shrubs to be trimmed. The incredible colors and fragrances of flowers.

I think of that first garden where life began.

I think of that final garden where Christ prayed. ("In my father's house are many mansions," he said. I feel sure that among those mansions there are many gardens too.)

How marvelous that man's existence—and woman's—began in a garden. Perhaps that's why we feel so wonderfully alive in a garden. And so close to you.

Needlework Prayer

Thank you for the joy of needlework, Lord. Though I sometimes wonder why I do it. All this time and money to fashion something I could buy far more easily . . . A canvas already painted, an already-woven cover or cushion or rug.

Yet here I sit persevering, inching toward the dream. Drawing these strands of color in and out, watching my own living fingers create the scene.

What deep secret drive impels me, Lord? So that I keep returning to my task, and when it is finished begin anew.

A love of beauty, yes, and the thrill of creating beautiful things. But more. For as I stitch away I feel *in* love, not only with this, my chosen pattern, but people too. My family, my friends, those who will eventually see this work and perhaps love it as well. But in a deeper sense—I love you.

I think of you whose canvas is the universe, and how tirelessly you make it beautiful for us. How you needlepoint the sky with stars, and cover the earth with fine little stitches of green. How you embroider the fields with flowers, and petit-point the beaches with sand and shells. I think of the brilliant, ever-changing tapestry of the trees.

Thank you for all this loveliness, Lord. For its patient artistry. When I take up my needle and thread the bright yarn, I feel very close to you.

The Cows

I don't need to seek God in nature, for he is there. Every sunrise testifies to his presence, every rainfall, every flower. It is impossible to stand by the sea and watch the waves rolling in without being almost overcome by a sense of his wonder, or see the wind lashing the trees without feeling his power.

And in nature I have learned lessons about God's own nature. They are written in the landscape, they are hidden yet ready to be discovered in the flight of birds or the very stance of trees. And secrets have been unlocked for me simply by observing his creatures, some of the answers to the eternal riddles of existence have been revealed.

I began to understand free will (at last!) on a creek bank one day, watching the cows. Five or six stood cooling themselves in the water, jaws busy, eyes bland. What a fixed stare cattle have. A kind of blank brooding. Their tails kept flicking flies off their backs, their jaws never ceased their silent rhythms. As we first approached, a couple of them emitted blasts of sound that sent the children scurrying. (A cow's moo is not a gentle thing, and musical only in stories.) Now they simply stood regarding me where I had stretched out on an army blanket.

The children were off trying to catch crawdaddies in a can. I lay alone resting, reading, gazing into the sky or returning the empty stare of the cows. . . . Overhead, clouds coasted, a hawk wheeled, and to the west I could glimpse a V of geese and faintly hear their honking. . . . How free the geese, I thought, how earth-bound and fated the cows.

Other birds called from the trees. What were they saying? I wondered. And what message had there been in the bellow of the cows? . . . Poor cows, blatting their foolish protests, now resignedly silent. Cows to be milked morning and night, or herded onto trucks and hauled off for slaughter. How sad to be a cow. If I had to be another creature and could choose, I'd join the wild geese flying. How free, how free! . : . But wait, the geese aren't free either. They fly always in formation and to certain feeding grounds at certain seasons. And their entire vocabulary is limited to that honking I hear faintly, thrillingly now. How sad to be a goose, speech-deprived.

And it occurs to me that human beings are the only creatures equipped with words. Why? Why were all the marvels of language reserved for us alone?

These cows. These birds. Not only the geese but the hobolinks singing from the pasture grasses, the turtle doves mourning, the other little voices chipper or sleepy in the trees . . . They are telling each other something, no doubt, they are expressing something. For almost every creature, bird or beast, has a voice with which to court, proclaim hunger, anger, fear, pain, and joy. And so, in a small and limited way they can communicate with each other and with us.

Yet they have no vocabulary, there is no way with which they translate their thoughts, if thoughts they have. They can't read, they can't write. They miss the entire experience of books and poetry and plays. . . . These books I have brought with me, to read or not. A cow couldn't choose; a bird could only peer over my shoulder, a butterfly poise on the pages, not understanding. Why should they? They have no need for the secrets locked in those letters.

The alphabet. Such a tiny package, less than a handful of letters to reveal such vast treasures: Words! Millions of words, not only in my own language but in the languages of the world. All but a few use this same alphabet. This magical key which I, as a person, own as a birthright and can use to my heart's delight. For I have been given the mind to understand it; and I have the sole choice what I shall speak, what I shall read, what I shall learn.

I can turn my back on knowledge and move dumbly through life like a cow, or I can open books and become transported in time and space. I can learn anything I want to in the whole wide world.

So as I lie in the shade beside that stream contemplating our differences—the cows' and mine, the birds' and mine—it dawns on me that herein lies the answer to something that long has troubled me: free will. In creating us as independent beings and sending us into life equipped with one simple tool God indeed made us "only a little lower than the angels." With dominion over the animals—and over ourselves.

That's it. That's got to be it!

For the animals aren't free. "Free as the birds," we say. Yet these very geese, flying in formation, are driven toward their destination by forces beyond their control. The bright singers in the trees—all, all function not from choice but from instinct. Even animals still living in the wild have been programmed to their ways, they needn't choose. Creatures of every other kind are trapped, usually within a single environment, during their brief life-span. Even their journeys, if they make them, are performed by instinct rather than choice, or by the choice of man. Animals can have neither dreams nor aspirations. They can't decide to work or not, or choose between the jobs they have (not even beavers or bees or ants). They can't invent things to make life easier. They can't benefit themselves by education; if they are trained at all, it is by man, and for the use and pleasure of man.

By comparison, how free we are. Trapped between birth and death, yes, but able to make so many choices in between. To do with our lives what we will. Average people—in a free society where there are no human dictators to force us—we can work where we please at whatever we please, marry whom we please, travel wherever we want.

Laws impose a few limits on us, there are social limits of our own devising, and we consider ourselves limited sometimes by lack of money or by the environment that seems wrong for us. But there is no force in existence that keeps us from breaking those limits, even of law. Unlike the animal kingdom, our Creator gave us free will. We can be as good or as bad as we want. As wise or as ignorant. We are free to move about and try things, accepting, rejecting, shaping the pattern of our days.

And when we are tempted to ask why God doesn't step in and intervene to spare us wars and murders and rapes, all the misfortunes that befall us, we must not forget that such intervention would be bought at the cost of forgoing our greatest gift of all.

We would then become as the animals. Free and yet not free. Free from the bother of making choices, from the penalties involved when we err. But herded about like cattle, dumb and wordless about our fate. Isn't it better, surely, to write the story of our own lives in a language freely given us? Our follies, our mistakes, the countless times of anguish caused by our very choices—surely even these are better than to live the bland life of a beast.

And this, too, has drawn me even closer to a personal reasoning God. If I could conceive of a universe populated only by animals—yes, it might possibly be considered some kind of mysterious, still awesome accident. . . .

But the fact that we, too, are here, Lord, your people thinking, speaking, laughing, choosing, falling, rising, loving—that can be no accident. Thank you for creating us in your image, releasing us on this remarkable planet with complete freedom to live the lives you have given us.

Music

Let me try to imagine a world without music. What if you'd given us such a world, God?

Not a silent world necessarily. Let it have the usual noises —sound of voices, pound of feet, bark of dogs . . . roar of engines, click of dishes and pans . . . bang of hammers and typewriter keys and doors. A busy, efficient world but a world without song . . . I can't bear it, the very concept is sad!

Not even bird song? No, this world empty of music would have to forgo even the belling and trilling of birds; only those with raucous cries could remain. . . . Not even a human whistler? No, because it's hard to whistle even at a girl without musical notes creeping in. Factory whistles, yes, calling people to work. Police whistles, traffic whistles, sirens—whistles for duty and danger. Shrill mechanical whistles—but no human whistles because when a person whistles he or she is glad.

And gladness would have little place in a world bereft of music. We would survive, I suppose. We would eat and sleep and work and mate and die. But would we love? Would we rejoice? Would we grieve? Would we be moved to acts of heroism or even acts of kindness? Would we achieve? . . . How could we? Why should we? For music is such an emotional thing. And doesn't everything in life circle round and round and in and out of us in rhythmic patterns of emotion?

Music stirs us, inspires us, uplifts our spirits or depresses them sometimes. ("Turn that off, it's too sad, I can't stand it!") Music charges our energies, our loyalties, our sense of pride—in a nation or a football team. (The flag is flying, here they come, listen to the band!) Music is "the food of love." We flirt to music, fall in love to music, dance, dream, and marry to music. From the lullabies sung at the cradle, to the taps that hurt so terribly, yet somehow make it all seem so right at the grave, music is inextricably entangled with our emotions. An outward expression of things we feel so deeply yet can't articulate.

How can anything so exquisite, so beautiful and powerful come from any source except the mysterious source of us all?

Come on somebody, show me. Dig up some proof, evolutionist; present me with some fact that will explain music. When and where in the meticulous selectivity of the species did music first begin? What manner of man first felt song stirring in his heart? Who or what put that yearning there and why? Who gave him the skill to express it? And where do the melodies come from?

Why the infinite variations, multiple as the stars, so that if you composed for a million years you could never exhaust the supply? . . . But no, there's no use trying to grasp the why and how of music, it is the most elusive art of all. A painting or piece of sculpture can be felt and touched. A book you can hold in your hand and read. But music?

Listen! . . . It comes to you across the hill, someone singing and playing. . . . It pours through your house from unseen sources (too many sometimes). . . . It may seem visible to you as the violinist moves his bow, the tympanist beats his drums, yet they are only the instruments; shut your eyes and you hear it in all its glory still. Even when you look at the score, you see only diagrams that the musician translates into these marvelous sounds. Sounds that somebody else first heard in his head . . . How come? Why did he hear them in the first place, and from where? And why, once these silent "sounds" have been set down on paper (and who can explain *that* transition?) and transposed by voice or instrument into what we call music, why should these sounds have any effect on *me?*

No, no, the mystery is too much. I give up, I can find no other source for it but God. No other *reason.* God must have given us music to sweeten life with its burdens, to give us an extra dimension for sharing life's emotions. Otherwise what *good* is it? And if it is good, then it is of God.

There must have been music before creation. (The music of the spheres.) There must have been music at the dawn of creation. And when man woke up and found himself upon the earth, I believe he must have heard the birds already singing and uttered his first song. And instinctively he must have reached out for a reed or stick with which to fashion an instrument to enhance and enlarge that song; to express greater feelings than his whistling lips or limited throat could.

The Bible is full of singing and playing . . . of lutes and timbrels and tabrets, of drums and flutes and harps and lyres. "The Jewish nation was a nation of musicians," says Henri Daniel-Rops. They must have music. Music to celebrate harvests and victories and feasts and weddings, music to mourn the dead. And to worship, ah, to worship! . . . David and his psalms. He could never have written those immortal words without the music that accompanied them, and he sang them to both Jehovah and King Saul. . . . The songs of Solomon could only have been born to music, and how much richer our heritage would be if we could know their original tunes. Music pulsates through the whole marvelous, fantastic story of man civilized and otherwise. Pagan, Jew or Christian, Moslem, Buddhist, Hindu, or American Indian, whatever the religion, music enables mortals to call out to the heavens from which we come. To make contact with our Creator. Music is the bridge sublime.

Isn't it significant that angels sang to announce the birth of Christ? "And suddenly with the angel there was a great throng of the heavenly host, praising God and singing: 'Glory to God in the highest heaven, and peace to men . . .'" (Luke

2:13–14, Jerusalem Bible). God himself turns to music. How else announce that tremendous event? Music, the universal language.

Music throughout the world. No words are needed when great music is played, no translators necessary. Attend an international youth orchestra festival. So many young people from so many countries, different in speech and face and dress. Yet when the conductor lifts his baton and the hands, black or white or brown, lift their instruments, all become as one. And when the strong sweet sounds begin to pour forth, all barriers vanish, the entire assemblage becomes as one. As one they hear and understand this common celestial tongue.

Who or what but an all-powerful common father could be back of such a phenomenon? This, too, a baptism of the Spirit . . .

To be able to hear music, what a blessing. But even the deaf don't miss it altogether. They, too, "hear" the pulsations, feel the rhythms, beat time, often dance. At Gallaudet, famous Washington college for the deaf, they have a robed choir and "sing" with their fingers! . . . The genius of Beethoven, overcoming even the deafness that began at thirty and was total by the time he was forty-nine. Imagine: to hear some of your own masterpieces only faintly, and that great oratorio *Missa Solemnis* not at all. Except in your mind . . .

Except in the mind . . . The miracle of the mind. What is mind but the unseen stuff of God? The ephemeral but potent dust of all creation drifting through our consciousness? Caught, held, transformed into ideas that are in turn transformed into things. Sometimes tangible things like houses and books and colleges and banks and cars. Sometimes that magnificent intangible, music.

How I'd love to be a composer, listening, ever listening for the sound of pianos and strings and brasses in my head, and when I heard them, able to set them down. I know it's not all that easy—but even to wrestle with the sounds, changing and rearranging until I had them meshed into near-perfection. How I'd love even to be a musician, drawing the music from a piano or horn or cello. . . . Observe musicians as they play. They are lost to us, they dwell in another world. They are transported to places where we cannot follow. They are close to the hearts of God.

As for us who sit listening . . . we are given glimpses of the divine. For a little while our own world changes, too, its harsh edges soften, melt into something lovely; the darks and the grays brighten, take on living colors; the grim gives way to something that shines. We are soothed or enlivened, delighted or profoundly moved. We forget, we forgive, we want to dance and laugh and love and cry.

Nobody can tell me this isn't your doing, God. Your very breath and being entering ours. Speaking to us, calling to us, using music to stir us, comfort us, uplift us. And giving us a foretaste of even more beautiful music to come.

Two by the Side
of the Road

*Jesus, dear Jesus, I sometimes envy you! When you felt
pity for people you had only to reach out and touch them
and they were healed. You could make them walk again,
you could restore their sight. . . . I feel such pity for
people, but so helpless before their plight. Jesus, dear
Jesus, show me what to do.*

The Good Samaritan. That parable was for all of us. That
parable was for me. . . . Oh, but it takes courage to be a
Good Samaritan, it can look silly, even be dangerous. It's not
safe to go to anybody's rescue any more, not even by daylight
on a busy street. New York, especially. People don't pay any
attention, just walk on by.

And I'm in New York now, taking a walk before a luncheon
appointment, on a bitterly cold day. And across the street, in
front of a funeral home, lies a body. Heavens, don't they even
pick up their *bodies?* Don't look, none of your business, hurry
on by. . . . But what if—? Never mind, look in store windows, beautiful clothes, forget that—*but what if it isn't a
body?* None of your business, don't be a hick. . . . Okay,
okay, cross the street, walk back just to be sure, it's probably
gone by now. . . . Only it isn't, and people are stepping
around it, paying no attention, although you see it moving,
hear its feeble cries—"Help me . . . some-body!" Okay, *okay,*
hick, chicken out-of-towner, break down, make a fool of yourself, ask what's the matter?

He's shaking, haggard, sick. He needs food, something

warm in his stomach. If you give him some money will he please go in out of the cold and eat? (You are begging for yourself!) He agrees, sobbing, and you hand him a dollar, escape. (Fool, he'll use it for drink.) When you look back he waves so plaintively you can't stand it. So go back, go back, idiot. "Your problem is alcohol, isn't it? Will you go to A.A. if I can get you there? They'll help you."

"Lady . . . I'll go . . . anywhere!"

Try to find a phone booth, try to find their number. They say they can't come after him, but if I can bring him by taxi . . . Try to get a taxi. . . . He is sitting up now, and another woman has stopped to talk to him. "Would you like for me to go with you?" she asks. Thank God. Especially since the headquarters prove to be in an undesirable section. (Could you have gotten him safely up those stairs by yourself, hick? Would the cab driver, sweet guy that he seemed to be, have helped you?) No matter, the other Good Samaritan supports his other side. . . . And they welcome him kindly, assure us he will have medical attention, food, a bed.

Leaving, the woman and I agree we, too, will sleep better tonight, knowing that. And that we could use some coffee ourselves. "He was worth saving," she says. "He's an educated man—did you notice his diction? And his manners, even so sick. When he said he'd never forget us he meant it. He's a good but very sick man."

Belatedly, we exchange names—and gasp. She is Ann Williams-Heller, well-known nutritionist. She writes for the same magazines I do, knows the same people! We fall into each other's arms, friends. . . . She came to this country as an Austrian war refugee. Now, years later, love brought us together. Out of all the people swarming the New York streets, the same life line from the same God drew us together at the side of someone who was suffering.

". . . whatsoever good thing any man doeth, the same shall he receive of the Lord. . . ."

It's not always that swift, that clear. Now I must record the incident of the old woman in Haifa, not to exalt myself, heaven knows, but only to try to understand the peculiar anguish of another love shared. . . .

She was bent over, heavy and stooped, with a homemade crutch under one arm, and in the other hand a knobby stick on which to lean. At her feet, a string bag filled with groceries. Evidently she had been shopping and discovered she could not carry them. She was weeping and making pitiful gestures to people thrusting past on the steep hot street.

I halted, torn. Our bus was making only a brief stop. Long enough to explore some of the art shops. I was rushing up the hill to look at some mosaics glimpsed in a window. But my heart would not let me pass. I halted, picked up the heavy bag, and tried to walk with her a little way.

Then I saw that her poor old feet in their run-over shoes could scarcely make it. She had to pause every few inches and point to one of them, so swollen it had broken through the thin flopping slipper. I set down the bag and knelt to examine it; the shoe was so broken and dusty it had rubbed the flesh raw. How to help, what to do? I tried putting a Kleenex in the sole to ease it a little bit. I caressed her foot with my fingers. Then I stood up and said, "Lean on me." And thus we progressed a little way.

Meanwhile, I was trying to enlist the aid of an Israeli soldier—anyone who might know where she lived and come to her aid. But if they understood they gave no sign; they simply shrugged and went on. All I could do was talk to her encouragingly in a language she did not understand. And when she had to stop again the hurt was too much for both of us, the love; I embraced her and kissed her and we clung together, so at least she realized that somebody cared. And she gazed at me through her tragic old eyes beneath the ragged shawl, and the tears flowed afresh.

The others were returning to the bus, calling, "Come on!" I would have to leave her. In desperation I hailed a boy of about fifteen and pleaded, "Do you speak English? Do you know where this woman lives? Can't you please carry her things home?" To my relief, he nodded, took up the bag, and set off down the hill. Behind him she continued to plod, inching along, halted again and again by the agonies of age. The last I saw was that stooped figure still making its tortuous way downhill in the blazing sun.

And my heart cried out after her. I felt as if I was abandoning her, as if I ought to give up all the comforts and joys of my own life to make her life easier . . . in that awful moment of recognition she was my mother! She was all the mothers who have borne children and grown old and crippled and live in poverty and torment as they struggle through their final days. I wanted to help her. I wanted to know that she lay on clean sheets in a cool house with somebody nearby to soothe her and keep her company.

I wanted to heal her. And to be able to do so little hurt so much.

I said that I sometimes envy Jesus. Now I realize . . . he couldn't heal everyone either, he couldn't provide for all the poor. There were simply too many. He, too, was limited by time and energy. And if *he* had limitations, how much greater are my human limitations. And if I suffer because of them, how much more he must have suffered for those people he had to turn away. (And must suffer still for us.)

But this I must remember. There were and are no limits on his love. All he asks of me is that I put no limits on my love.

Flying Through Fog

I can barely see the wings, Lord, but they are outspread like arms. Like your everlasting arms.

They hold us up, they reach out like a benediction. "Don't be afraid," they say, and so do the bright little lights. "We are strong, we are firm."

I see the small flaps open and close as we speed steadily forward through the fog. They are like the movements of an enigmatic but reassuring smile.

I am relaxed, I am calm. Who can fear the clouds and the fog which surround us like the very breath of God?

Like homing pigeons we are being led to our destination. Blindly yet surely the instruments lead us home.

Your hand is upon us, your eye is upon us. Though we rise and fall with the currents—on this journey or through the fogs of life, you will hold us up. You will see us through. We reach firm ground, we land.

Oh, Lord, let me remember this later, at the times when I need it, when the fogs of life overtake me and there seems to be no landing place—let me remember this flight through the fog.

Poetry

Poetry . . . its rhythms that echo the rhythms of the universe. This, too, speaks to me of God.

In the beginning, the very beginning, a mother rocking her child to sleep—the songs she croons to him, the little nonsense chantings. All this cradling and loving—there is heartbeat back of it all—her own heartbeat and the great heartbeat of God.

With some of us, once this rhythm begins it never ceases; from Mother Goose to Masefield, we respond. From the little gooseboy wandering "upstairs and downstairs, and in my lady's chamber" to Masefield going "down to the sea in ships . . ." And the sea itself rolls in, the waves never varying their patterns. The very wind cries in cadences, and the trees turn into lovely swaying poems in the wind. While the rain pounds out its measures on the roof.

God puts a hunger in some hearts when we are very small; God puts a pencil in the hand. There is no appeasing that hunger unless the pencil moves, too, struggling with these elusive rhythms.

God, and a good librarian, led me to poetry in the wonderful library we had in Storm Lake, my little home town. The poetry books were few, but their treasures overwhelming. Here it had happened, the miracle had happened—the words had been shaped to their delicate true purpose, people had captured the wind!

God led me to the Psalms. . . . I remember almost the very moment as a child in church one morning. The responsive reading. From the pulpit a voice leading: "Thou crownest the year with thy goodness; and thy paths drop fatness." And we, all of us, even those new to the wonder of words, could reply: "They drop upon the pastures of the wilderness: and the little hills rejoice on every side."

The little hills! . . . And the rest: "The pastures are clothed with flocks; the valleys also are covered over with corn; they shout for joy, they also sing."

Something shouted for joy within me, too; the Holy Spirit roused me through this poem. . . . And today, reading the Psalms today, whatever our age, we walk again on hillsides clothed with flocks and corn, and love God and challenge God and bow down before the mystery and the marvel of his never-ending plan.

For the universe, the whole universe, is one great poem. Day and night, birth and death, winter and spring, blossoming and withering, sunshine and storm . . . the metronome swings, the very stars in their courses have such meter they could be scanned.

And even when God himself seems to have gotten lost somewhere, or we have wandered off like the little boy in Mother Goose and can't be found—we have not been banished, and there is no banishing the patterns. The language of the world is never stilled, the great eternal system with its tireless heart pounds on.

And so poetry is of God. True poetry that makes one's own heart leap in recognition. Reading it, poetry that some other tormented or rhythm-rejoicing soul has brought into being, is sometimes as if God himself has struck us down unaware from the printed page.

Yes, oh yes—this is another way to be hurled straight into the heart of God.

With the Tongues
of Men and Angels

Jesus said: "Thou shalt love the Lord thy God with all thy heart, and with all thy soul, and with all thy mind. That is the first and great commandment. And the second is like unto it, Thou shalt love thy neighbor as thyself."

The thirteenth chapter of First Corinthians tells us how. The famous chapter on charity, or love. And how that Paul could write! No author, not even Shakespeare, has ever produced anything to surpass that treatise. "Though I speak with the tongues of men and of angels, and have not love, I am become as sounding brass, or a tinkling cymbal."

Read it, oh read it to learn the true nature of love. Some versions use the word *charity;* no matter, the words are interchangeable, they mean the same thing. (And how significant that is.) Generosity, giving, sharing, having mercy, being patient, showing compassion, understanding. And no matter what I say, or how many people I help, if I go about this bitterly or grudgingly, then "it profiteth me nothing." If I am truly to know and love God, I must have love for his people in my heart.

This means I will be charitable in my spirit as well as my acts. I will refrain from judgments. ("Judge not, that ye be not judged. . . ." Who knows what agony lies behind the locked doors of another person's life?) I will not stone a brother or sister with words. ("Inasmuch as ye have done it unto one of the least of these my brethren, ye have done it unto me.")

I will love my neighbors, and show it whenever I can even though I may not tell them so. I will try to love my God with all my heart and soul and mind—and *tell* him so.

For the very words of love enhance and intensify love. If I want to find God and hang on to him, I've got to thank him for creating me and letting me live. Every moment of my life will be a witness to that wonder. But he will be closer, ever closer, if I love him and tell him so!

"And now abideth all these things . . ." that have helped lead me back to God.

People and writings and work. Birth and death and nature. The church and prayer and pain and the wonders of art.

"*. . . but the greatest of these is love.*"

When the Winds Cry I Hear You

Oh, God, my God, when the winds cry I hear you, when the birds call I hear you, when the sea rushes in it is like the rushing of my being toward yours.

You are voice of wind and bird and beat of sea. You are the silent steady pulsing of my blood.

I would know you better, I would taste your essence, I would see your face.

Yet these few small senses of mine cannot do more. You have defined their limits, you have set them within a framework from which we can only see and touch and hear and attempt to know these marvels that you have made.

But this too is the marvel—that you are within each of us as well. As we are drawn toward your greatness we are drawn toward the greatness within ourselves.

We are larger beings, we are greater spirits.

The hunger for you kindles a holy fire that makes us kinder, gentler, surer, stronger—ever seeking, never quite finding, but always keenly aware that you are all about us and within us.

You are here.

ABOUT THE AUTHOR

Few women writing today have touched the lives of as many people as has MARJORIE HOLMES. She has been described by *The New York Times* as "an American phenomenon" and by the *Washington Post* as "the housewives' patron saint." Her best-selling books include *Hold Me Up a Little Longer, Lord; How Can I Find You, God?; Nobody Else Will Listen; Who Am I, God?; I've Got to Talk to Somebody, God* and *Two from Galilee*.

Heartwarming Books
of
Faith and Inspiration